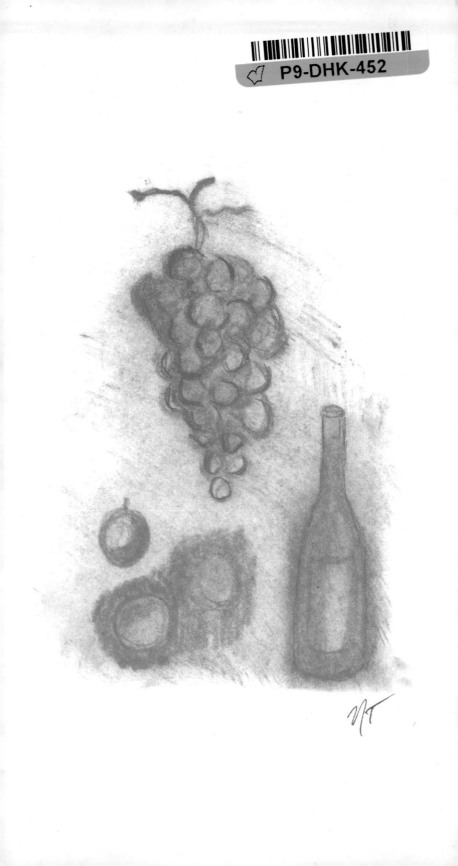

# Discovering Maryland Wineries

## A Travel Guide to Maryland's Wine Country

By Kevin M. Atticks

**resonant ◉ publishing**

resonant publishing
Baltimore, Maryland

Printed in the United States of America by
Data Reproductions Corporation, Auburn Hills, Michigan.
This book is printed on acid-free paper.


Library of Congress Catalog Card Number:  98-89112
ISBN:  0-9668716-0-X



First Edition, updated
10  9  8  7  6  5  4  3  2  1



Cover photo by Kevin M. Atticks
Back cover sketch by Nickitas B. A. Thomarios
Cover and interior design by resonant design
Edited by Judy Dobler




**resonant◉publishing**

Baltimore, Maryland
www.resonantgroup.com

This book is dedicated to
June Atticks,
who taught me to
love unconditionally and
to always believe in myself.

*Good wine
is a necessity of life for me.*

—Thomas Jefferson

# Table of Contents

Acknowledgements................................................................iv
Introduction ......................................................................1
History of Maryland Wine.......................................................4
Things to Know Before You Go!................................................10
Map of Maryland Wineries.....................................................12

## Maryland Wineries and Vineyards

Basignani Winery...............................................................14
Boordy Vineyards...............................................................20
Catoctin Vineyards .............................................................26
Cygnus Wine Cellars ..........................................................32
Deep Creek Cellars............................................................38
Elk Run Vineyards and Winery ..............................................44
Fiore Winery....................................................................50
Linganore Winecellars at Berrywine Plantation..........................56
Loew Vineyards ................................................................62
Woodhall Vineyards and Wine Cellars......................................68
Maryland Grape Growers......................................................74

## Mason-Dixon Wine Trail Wineries

Introduction ....................................................................80
Map of Wine Trail .............................................................81
Allegro Vineyards (PA)........................................................82
Naylor Vineyards and Wine Cellar (PA) ...................................86
Seven Valleys Vineyard (PA) ................................................90

## Good Information

Wine Festivals..................................................................96
Wine Associations..............................................................97
Wine Publications..............................................................98
Where to Buy Maryland Wines ..............................................99
Useful Wine Terms ...........................................................100
Order Form/More Info .......................................................102

# Acknowledgements

The following people have provided me with invaluable
information during the preparation of this book:
Anthony and Lucille Aellen, Linganore Winecellars
Eric Fiore, Fiore Winery
Jack and Emily Johnston, Copernica Vineyards
Kim Rose & Steve Olko, Data Reproductions Corporation
Paul Roberts, Deep Creek Cellars
Al Spoler, WJHU's *Cellar Notes*
Muphen Whitney, Association of Maryland Wineries

The following people deserve special recognition, for their
friendship and guidance have meant much more than they know:
Ralph and Terry Atticks
Jan Buhrmann
Andy Ciofalo
Ashlea Clark
Mary DeManss
Judy Dobler
Sarah Drury
John McGraw
George Miller
John Mohan
Karen Neilson
David Rittenhouse
Diane DeLisa Willian
Tom Yulsman

Thanks to each winemaker, their family and staff for being so
patient and cooperative—especially during harvest!

Art and sketches by Nickitas B. A. Thomarios
Maps provided by Brian Schumacher
Photographs by Kevin M. Atticks
Edited by Judy Dobler

*Wine is proof that God loves us
and wants to see us happy.*

—Benjamin Franklin

# Introduction

Maryland wineries have much to offer wine aficionados and curious first-timers alike. They're a lot closer than Napa Valley or Bordeaux, and their wines are much more unique. All but one of the Maryland wineries are within two hours from Washington and Baltimore. They are easily reached and well worth the drive.

I set out to write this book for one simple reason: I love Maryland wine. To be honest, it took a trip to California for me to realize that Maryland even had a history of grape growing and winemaking. A winemaker at a well-known winery in Sonoma Valley told me that some of his first vines came from Philip Wagner in Maryland. Wagner, he said, was the grandfather of American wine.

As it turns out, winemakers throughout the world know Wagner and his work. I soon found out that Wagner imported some vinifera and hybrid vines from France to the United States and began a nursery just north of Baltimore. This nursery was eventually transformed into Boordy Vineyards, one of Maryland's foremost wineries.

I was not home from California a week before I had visited Linganore Winecellars, my first Maryland winery. The wine and the people were lots of fun! I thought it was a fluke, so they told me to drive up the road to Loew Vineyards. Again, I was greeted with wonderful wine. Just 1.5 miles away at Elk Run Vineyards I found superb wine once again. Much to my surprise and enjoyment, the quality of the wine was outstanding and each winery had a style all its own. The winemakers of Maryland are making many popular varieties of wine while creating others rarely seen in other regions.

I want to encourage you to seek out our local wineries and discover their spectacular wines. This book is meant to make you aware of Maryland's wineries, to introduce you to the people who run them, and to give you an idea of what to expect when you visit.

The book is designed to make it easy for you to find out everything you need to know before you go to the wineries. Each winery is described in its own chapter (deservedly so!) enabling you to focus on one winery at a time. On the second page of each chapter are directions and a map showing you where the winery is in relation to the major roads that will get you there. Check to see which wineries are located near each other, as it's nice to visit more than one at a time!

At the end of each chapter I've listed the wines you can expect to find at each winery (with the exception of seasonal wines). I've left a bit of space for you to write your thoughts on each wine after tasting it. This is an invaluable exercise—many times you'll try to remember the who, what, where, and when of a wine: taking notes is the easiest way to keep track of your favorites.

Each winery has a different style and approach to winemaking. Every one has a completely different feel. If you are interested in classic Italian wines, then Fiore is the answer. If Bordeaux and California wines are your style, then be sure to stop by Catoctin. If you're interested in superb wines that have won the acclaim of wine writer Robert Parker Jr., head to Basignani. For extremely good table wines at great prices, make the drive to Deep Creek Cellars. For fun wines and great festivals, make your way to Linganore Winecellars.

I encourage you to visit all wineries, not because I'm their biggest fan, but because each one offers an entirely unique perspective on the art of winemaking. You need not enjoy every wine from every winery. Chances are you probably won't, since the styles are so varied and unique.

As I mentioned before, try to visit a few wineries at a time, so you are armed with fresh memories. This will enrich your visits and give you perspective when evaluating all the wines you'll try.

It's not unreasonable to tour all the wineries in a weekend, although the stretch of road between Fiore Winery in Harford County and Deep Creek Cellars is fairly expansive. It may be a good idea to break your visits up into groups of three or four wineries at a time. Or, take a weekend to visit one winery and some of the surrounding attractions. Many of the attractions are educational, while some are pure pleasure (like antique shopping in New Market or tubing the Gunpowder River).

The most important aspect of this book is that it be informative. It exposes a side of Maryland's agriculture that can only be described as the perfect combination of skill and art. And all along, it was right here in our backyards.

## *Enjoy!*

# History of Maryland Wine

Contributed by Jack Johnston
Maryland Grape Growers Association

The earliest recorded instance of winemaking in Maryland was that of Tenis Palee, who made wines from native American grapes in 1648. They are reported to have had high alcohol and strong flavors. In 1662, Governor Charles Calvert, at the prompting of Lord Baltimore, planted 200 acres on the east bank of St. Mary's River, using vines he had received from several countries in Europe. These were later supplemented by another 100 acres. Most failed to survive. Other colonists imported vines during the next century, but again not enough survived to allow wine to be made in any significant quantity.

The only grape of quality to appear was 'Alexander,' presumably a natural hybrid of a wild native vine with one of the imported European (vinifera) varieties. Benjamin Tasker Jr. planted two acres in 1756 in what is now Prince George's County and made a passable red wine.

Charles Carroll planted a vineyard in Howard County in 1768. It included some natural hybrids and some European varieties, but by 1800 all but the indigenous vines died. Other interspecific varieties continued to appear in the 19th century, but the wine made from them was never a match for European quality. John Adler made wine from Alexander in Havre de Grace around 1800—it was well-received—and later he propagated 'Catawba,' another hybrid that proved better than the Alexander.

In 1823 Adler wrote the first American book on viticulture and winemaking, which encouraged others to grow grapevines, and in 1829 the Maryland Society for Promoting the Culture of the Vine was formed. The society had limited success, but most of their vineyard efforts were plagued by severe winter temperatures and fungus diseases.

Shortly thereafter, these diseases made their way to Europe and

proceeded to devastate most of the vineyards there. An intense effort to identify the nature of these diseases resulted in the development of fungicide sprays such as Bordeaux mix (copper/lime). These fungicides, along with grafting quality varieties onto native American rootstocks which are more disease resistant, make it possible to grow the European varieties in the eastern United States today.

In the early part of the 20th century a number of hybridizers in France were producing crosses between native American and traditional European varieties. The resulting varieties retained the native resistance to disease and sub-zero temperatures while allowing for improved character.

In the early forties, Philip Wagner, then an editorial columnist with the Baltimore *Sun* and later editor of the *Evening Sun*, acquired as many different hybrids as he could lay hands on and planted them at his home in Riderwood. The success of his efforts signaled a turning point in the eastern wine industry. In addition to making his own wine, he propagated the vines and sold them throughout the east coast. He opened Boordy Vineyards, Maryland's first bonded winery, in 1945, producing wines made from the hybrid grapes. Most were simple, easy-to-drink wines, designated simply 'red' or 'white'—it was his philosophy that the winemaker's goal should be to make inexpensive everyday wines for consumption with meals.

Wagner also produced the first up-to-date wine-making text, *American Wines and How to Make Them*, which was later revised as *Grapes Into Wine* and has become a classic in the field. He also wrote *A Wine Growers Guide*, which has remained a staple in the vineyard establishment repertoire.

In the years that followed, fifteen additional wineries opened, of which eight are still functioning. In 1954, Charles Singleton, a Johns Hopkins Humanities professor who grew grapes for Wagner, started his own winery, Caroli Vineyard, using hybrid grapes. His efforts strongly influenced Dr. G. Hamilton Mowbray, a research psychologist at Applied Physics Laboratory at Johns Hopkins, who was planting several varieties of hybrids acquired from Singleton. When Caroli closed in 1962, Dr. Mowbray decided to open his own winery, and in 1966 Montbray Wine Cellars became the third bonded winery in Maryland. In addition to the hybrids, Mowbray produced Cabernet Sauvignon, Chardonnay, and Riesling, and in 1974 he produced Maryland's first ice wine, made from Riesling. He in turn became the major influence on most of the winemakers who followed him into the commercial wine business. Both he and Philip Wagner received the prestigious Merite Agricole award from the French Embassy. He retired in 1994.

Most of the wineries which opened over the next few decades were family operations, managed by people in their spare time while holding down other full-time jobs. Tom Provenza, an orthodontist, opened a winery in 1974 in Montgomery County, producing red and white hybrid blends. The winery closed in 1983, due to the owner's ill health.

Bret and Sharon Byrd opened Byrd Winery near Mt. Airy in 1976, concentrating on vinifera varieties—Cabernet, Chardonnay, Riesling, and Sauvignon Blanc. The winery closed in 1996, although a subsequent harvest was taken by Boordy Vineyards.

Ira Ross opened Bon Sporonza Winery in Westminster that same year, producing mostly hybrids and fruit wines, several of them packaged in bag-in-the-box containers. The winery closed in 1982.

The Aellen family started Linganore Winecellars at Berrywine Plantation in 1976 on a farm north of Mt. Airy, producing French hybrids, native American, dry and sweet fruit wines, and some flavored wines such as sangria and mead. Jack Aellen was responsible for establishing Maryland's first viticulture region, designated 'Linganore.' The 'Catoctin' region was designated shortly thereafter, followed a few years later by the 'Cumberland Valley.'

In 1977 Bob and Ruth Ziem opened Ziem Wine Cellars near Downsville, using exclusively hybrid grapes and concentrating heavily on red varieties. The winery closed in 1998 with Bob's retirement.

When Philip Wagner retired in 1980, Boordy Winery was sold to the Deford family in Hydes. During the next several years, Rob Deford greatly expanded the scope of the operation, adding new varieties, including viniferas and enlarging the facilities and the vineyards. Boordy introduced Maryland's first commercial sparkling wine in 1989.

Some noteworthy research was done in cloning grapevines during the mid-1970s. Bill Krul at the U. S. Department of Agriculture succeeded in producing a viable grapevine using somatic embryo genesis. Additional experimentation was done by John McGrew at the USDA in Beltsville and by Ham Mowbray, who still maintains a small vineyard of Seyval clones.

By the mid-1970s, the severely restrictive Maryland laws governing wine, which limited production and sales at the wineries, began to ease, due to the lobbying efforts of the winery owners. This opened the way for the establishment of a number of new wineries.

In 1983, Al Copp and Mike DeSimone opened Woodhall Vineyards and Wine Cellars in Baltimore County, producing Cabernet Sauvignon, Chardonnay, and a number of hybrids. Operations were curtailed with Mike's untimely death in 1987, but fully restored when Chris and Pat Lang became Al's new partners in 1991. A new vineyard was established at the Lang residence, in addition to which another vineyard nearby is currently maintained by Woodhall.

Also in 1983, Jerry and Ann Milne, along with Bob Lyon, a former Byrd winemaker, opened Catoctin Vineyards in Brookeville, using grapes from an already established vineyard which now comprises nearly thirty acres, and using the winery facilities formerly owned by Provenza. The wines are mostly vinifera, including Cabernet Sauvignon, Cabernet Franc, Chardonnay, and Riesling. The vineyard is now managed by Boordy.

The same year saw Fred and Carol Wilson's Elk Run Winery in operation, initially using exclusively vinifera varieties. In addition to a new vineyard recently planted on their site near Mt. Airy, the Wilsons currently manage a portion of the former Montbray vineyards.

In 1984, lawyer Fooks Truitt produced both vinifera and hybrid wines—all whites and rosés—from vines planted in 1981 at his

Whitemarsh Cellars winery near Westminster. The winery closed a few years later.

Bill and Lois Loew opened Loew Vineyards in 1985, producing both vinifera and hybrid wines. Some of the wines are blends of the two types, but varietals are produced as well.

Bert Basignani, a longtime amateur winemaker, turned professional in 1986 with Basignani Winery. He produces both vinifera and hybrid wines, including an occasional Merlot, a rarity in Maryland.

Mike and Rose Fiore opened Fiore Winery in 1987 in Harford County, and their winery and vineyard have expanded rapidly ever since. Standard vinifera and hybrid varieties are produced along with several proprietary blends.

In 1981, the Maryland Grape Growers Association was formed. The primary purpose of the organization at that time was to support the Maryland wine industry by encouraging commercial growers. Since then, its perspective has broadened to include many small-scale, 'backyard' vineyardists, many of whom sell their produce to amateur winemakers. MGGA produces a quarterly newsletter and a vineyard establishment manual and sponsors several on-site activities during the year.

The Association of Maryland Wineries was founded in 1984, the purpose of which was to coordinate winery activities and deal with legal and commercial issues involving the production and distribution of Maryland wines. Currently, the association is actively engaged in pursuing legislation to hasten the growth of the winemaking and grape growing industries in the state, and is focusing on ways to promote the broader use of Maryland wines by Marylanders.

That same year, the first Maryland Wine Festival was held at the Union Mills Homestead in Carroll County. All Maryland wineries participated, and its success led to its establishment as an annual two day event at the Carroll County Farm Museum. The local chapter of the American Wine Society sponsors amateur wine judgings, wine education seminars, and wine-making demonstrations, and the Maryland Grape Growers Association dispenses grape juice and provides grape growing information.

In subsequent years, other wine festivals have emerged in Howard, Harford, and Baltimore counties and in Annapolis. The burgeoning attention to local wines and the recognition of the industry as a potential major factor in the tourism industry led to the formation of the Maryland Winery and Grape Growers Advisory Board. Its function is to advise the Secretary of Agriculture on economic and legal issues regarding the state wine and grape growing industries. The MWGGAB also solicits and recommends the use of resources for marketing, education, and enological and viticultural projects deemed essential for promoting growth in the industry.

The most serious problem currently facing the Maryland wine industry is the severe shortage of grapes. The wineries are permitted to buy out-of-state fruit, but the situation is no better in neighboring states. Most wineries maintain their own vineyards, more from necessity than choice, since the commercial growers cannot provide the quantities needed to allow expansion and diversity. MGGA has stepped up efforts to recruit new growers, but it takes years to produce a crop and the short-term prospects are not encouraging.

In spite of this problem, two new wineries—Cygnus Wine Cellars in Carroll County, owned by Ray Brasfield, and Deep Creek Cellars in Garrett County, owned by Paul Roberts—opened in 1997; two other wineries are in the planning or formation stages on Maryland's eastern shore.

Maryland's grape growers harvest an average of 450 tons a year. The wineries produce more than 300,000 bottles of wine a year, with annual sales of nearly $2 million.

# Things to Know Before You Go!
*(or, things I learned while writing this book!)*

1.  Give yourself ample time and don't schedule anything else to do the day of your visits. The whole idea of a winery is to stop in, talk, tour, and try some wine (and hopefully BUY, BUY, BUY when you find something you like!!). The people who greet you in the winery more than likely either own the wineries or make the wine, so spend some time talking and asking questions. You might even make some new friends.

2.  Dress comfortably. None of the wineries are formal. Or even semiformal. Plus, with Maryland's warm swampy weather half the year, you will want to be comfortable and relaxed!

3.  Bring friends and family along. It's much more fun to visit the wineries in small groups. Kids are welcome, too!

4.  Don't be afraid to try all the wines. Maybe you only like reds. Maybe you only like whites. Maybe you only like Dr Pepper. Even though you may think you only like one type of wine, try all the wines available for tasting—you may find that your tastes have evolved. Keep an open mind. Besides, most wineries offer free tastings so it's no loss to you!

5.  Take notes. I've included a wine list in each chapter with space for notes. Don't worry about wine lingo. If a wine smells like pears, pineapples, or blackberries, say so. If it tastes like diesel fuel, potting soil, or a wet saddle, say so—you may be on to something! It's not necessary to like every wine tried, but it's a good idea to record your likes and dislikes for future reference.

6.  Bring cash (although most take personal checks and credit, too!) to purchase your favorites. You'll probably find something at each winery that grabs your attention. Don't worry—Maryland wine is very fairly priced. The quality you get from a small Maryland winery often meets or beats much of what you can find for the same price from California.

7.  Plan on buying at least one bottle of wine at each winery. All of the wineries covered in this book are relatively small, and they count on tasting room sales to make money. All have wine priced under $10 so consider it a common courtesy to purchase a bottle at each, although I can almost guarantee you'll find something worth buying at each!

8.  Take advantage of the local attractions. Just because the winery is a little out of the way doesn't mean it's in the middle of nowhere.

9.  Pace yourself and don't overdo it. If you're going to hit a few wineries in one day, make sure you stop to eat in between, lest you walk into the next winery with blurry eyes. It's always a good idea to pack a picnic lunch, and most wineries have picnic areas where you're free to munch.

10.  ENJOY YOURSELF!! The best part about touring the wineries is meeting fun people and tasting their spectacular wines. As a friend once told me, "I've never had a bad wine with friends." I agree, and I hope you will too!

# Map of Maryland Wineries

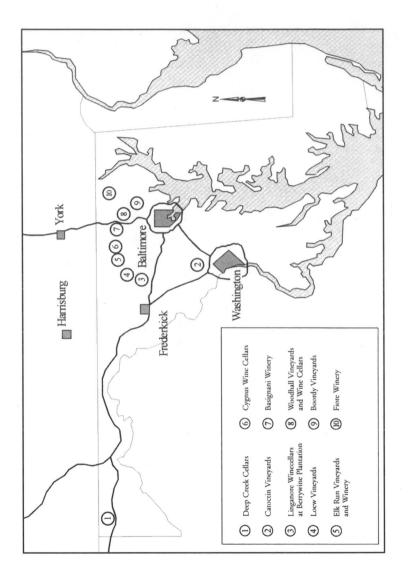

| | | | |
|---|---|---|---|
| ① | Deep Creek Cellars | ⑥ | Cygnus Wine Cellars |
| ② | Catoctin Vineyards | ⑦ | Basignani Winery |
| ③ | Linganore Winecellars at Berrywine Plantation | ⑧ | Woodhall Vineyards and Wine Cellars |
| ④ | Loew Vineyards | ⑨ | Boordy Vineyards |
| ⑤ | Elk Run Vineyards and Winery | ⑩ | Fiore Winery |

# Maryland Wineries

*Wine improves with age.*
*The older I get, the better I like it.*

—*Anonymous*

# BASIGNANI WINERY

| | |
|---|---|
| Founded: | 1986 |
| Owners: | Bert and Lynn Basignani |
| Winemakers: | Bert Basignani; Mike Vinzant, cellar master |
| Address: | 15722 Falls Road |
| | Sparks, MD 21152 |
| Phone: | (410) 472-4718 |
| Hours: | Saturdays 12-5 p.m. and Sundays 1-5 p.m. |
| | Tours and tastings are free. |
| Annual production: | 3,000 gallons |
| Price range of wines: | $7.90 to $22.00 |
| Amenities available: | Bathrooms, picnic areas. The winery is wheelchair accessible. |
| Area Wineries: | Boordy Vineyards |
| | Woodhall Vineyards and Wine Cellars |
| Local attractions: | NCR Hike and Bike Trail |
| | Gunpowder River (Lynn suggests tubing it after visiting the winery.) |
| | Oregon Ridge Park |

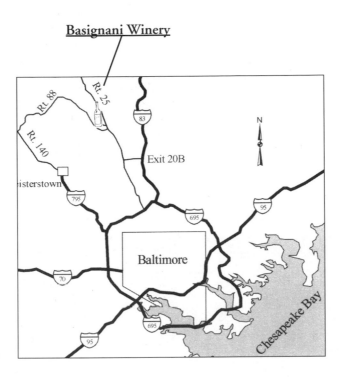

**Basignani Winery**

## Directions:

From Baltimore: Take I-83 north to Shawan Road west (20B). Go three miles to Falls Road and turn right. Go approximately six miles north, passing Blackrock Road (Route 88). Look for the winery sign on the left. Go up the driveway and take the first left into the Basignani's driveway.

From Washington: Take I-95 north to I-695 west towards Towson. Take I-83 north to Shawan Road exit (20B) and head west. Go three miles to Falls Road and turn right. Go approximately six miles north, passing Blackrock Road (Route 88). Look for the winery sign on the left. Go up the driveway and take the first left into the Basignani's driveway.

After the wooded drive on Falls Road, you'll be glad when you finally see the winery on the left. Take the driveway to the first house on the left and park just up the hill. Just to the right is the winery—half barn, half garage—which sits just across from the Basignani's house.

For Bert and Lynn Basignani, family is everything. Elena, Marisa, and Lorenzino are three of Basignani's children and happen to be their best wines, and if you're lucky, you may get to meet their inspiration. Their oldest son, Eric, has been waiting long enough for a wine of his own. If you've got any ideas, Lynn and Bert are taking suggestions.

Behind the winery the vines stand in perfect rows up a smooth hill (makes for great sunsets). Bert planted his first grapes in 1975,

*Bert Basignani positions the tractor to pick-up grapes during harvest.*

and Basignani Winery was bonded in 1986. "We started out with French hybrids from Boordy and have since expanded," says Bert. They've expanded to a total of eleven acres of vines and are trying new varieties to test their performance on site.

The Basignanis are currently growing Chardonnay, Riesling, Cabernet Sauvignon, Merlot, Foch, Burdin, Chambourcin, Chancellor,

Seyval, and Vidal. They offer ten wines made from these grapes at any given time, giving wine-lovers a choice of styles and tastes.

Because this is a family operation, every fall there's a call for volunteers to harvest. "People come from all over to help us harvest," Lynn says. And Lynn is known for the great lunch she puts together for volunteer grape-pickers. "Harvesting is hard work: volunteers deserve a big thanks," Lynn says.

Both Lynn and Bert hold full-time jobs, working the vines and vats on weekends. Bert plans to jump into wine-making full time in the near future. "It's a lot of work for the weekends," he says, but explains how the wines are worth the effort. Reknowned wine critic Robert Parker Jr. rated Basignani's 1993 Lorenzino Reserve 88 points out of 100 and has mentioned their Chardonnay as one of Maryland's best.

# Uniquities:

- wines have been rated favorably by Robert Parker Jr.
- wines must be good (they're named after the Basignani's children)
- quick hop from Baltimore

Bert and Lynn aren't the only ones you'll meet at Basignani winery. Gatsby, the Basignani's Border Collie and his new bride Daisy, are usually out and about on the grounds, tending to business, but are always in the mood for affection. Very suspicious at first, Gatsby befriends anyone who will throw pine cones, sticks, or anything feasibly fetchable.

Basignani winery is just minutes north of Oregon Ridge, making it a great place to stop before an event at the park. Check with the winery to find out about their special events including a holiday open house the weekend after Thanksgiving and the first weekend in December.

# ine List

Johannisberg Riesling

Elena

Vidal

Chardonnay

Seyval

Lorenzino Reserve

Cabernet Sauvignon

Marisa

# $\mathcal{R}$ecipes

## Lynn's Penne Pasta with Fresh Tomatoes and Mozzarella

Marinate fresh, peeled, cut-up roma tomatoes in a large ceramic bowl with the following: olive oil, chopped garlic, fresh basil, and cubed mozzarella.

Get ready ahead of time and let marinate for several hours.
Cook penne rigate and when al dente, add to bowl and mix together. Add salt and pepper to taste.

Serve with Basignani Elena.

## Kevin's Portobello Mushroom Chowder

| | |
|---|---|
| 2 large portobello mushrooms | 1 clove of garlic |
| 2 medium yellow onions, diced | |
| | |
| 1 quart of oat or soy milk | 4 tbsp flour |
| 2 tbsp soy sauce | 1 tbsp nutmeg |
| 3 tbsp virgin olive oil | Salt and pepper to taste |

Begin with the broth. In a medium pot, heat the oat or soy milk until hot but not boiling. Add flour and stir to thicken. Add olive oil and then soy sauce and nutmeg to your liking while stirring.

Dice the onions and garlic and cut the portobello mushrooms into long slices or into squares. Add the onions, garlic and mushrooms to the broth and bring to boil for five minutes. Take off heat and serve. Serves 2-3.

Serve with Basignani Vidal or Marisa.

*(The first recipe was submitted by Lynn Basignani of Basignani winery. The second was submitted by the author.)*

# BOORDY VINEYARDS

| | |
|---|---|
| Founded: | 1945 |
| Owners: | R. B. Deford Family Proprietors |
| Winemaker: | Tom Burns |
| Address: | 12820 Long Green Pike |
| | Hydes, MD 21082 |
| Phone: | (410) 592-5015 |
| WWW: | www.boordy.com |
| Hours: | Monday thru Saturday 10-5 p.m., Sunday 1-5 p.m. Daily tours are free for groups of fewer than 10 and are are given 1-4 p.m. on the hour. Groups of 10 or more should call ahead. |
| Annual production: | 24,000 gallons |
| Price range of wines: | $5.75 to $18.00 |
| Amenities available: | Picnic tables and bathrooms are available. |
| Area Wineries: | *"Mason-Dixon Wine Trail"* Wineries |
| | Basignani Winery |
| Local attractions: | Ladew Topiary Gardens |
| | Hampton Mansion |
| | Gunpowder Falls State Park |

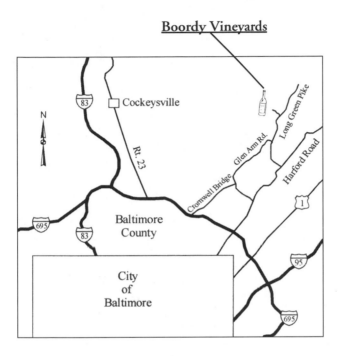

**Boordy Vineyards**

## Directions:

From the Baltimore Beltway (I-695): Take exit 29 (Cromwell Bridge Road) and go left 2.9 miles to the end. Turn left onto Glen Arm Road and continue 3.2 miles to the intersection with Long Green Pike. Turn left and go two miles; you'll see the winery's entrance on the left. Park in front of the winery housed in the large stone and wood barn to the left, down the hill.

As one of the best known wineries in Maryland, Boordy has a lot to live up to. The winery is located just north of Baltimore in Long Green Valley, where half of their grapes are grown. Fifty-three years in the making, Boordy has expanded in size and popularity beyond anyone's aspirations since being founded in 1945 by Philip and Jocelyn Wagner.

Wagner was a pioneer grape grower and actually smuggled some hybrid vines back to the United States after his stay in France as a Baltimore *Sun* reporter. Wagner later published *American Wines and How to Make Them* in 1933, a book that made him known and respected around the country—it was the only book of its kind written in English at the time.

The Wagners envisioned making affordable, accessible wines for everyday people. The Deford family, longtime family friends of the Wagners, bought the winery in 1980 and have consistently continued the Wagner's winemaking vision.

*Boordy's tasting room extends outside on nice days!*

Robert Deford III has been continuing the Boordy tradition by continually introducing innovative practices and products, while winemaker Tom Burns keeps very busy with Boordy's diverse selection of wines.

The tasting room, located in the large stone and wood winery barn, is quaint but roomy enough for a few tasters at a time. Although once inhabited by cows, the 19th century barn serves a more stately duty as Boordy's winecellar as well. The barn's second level is now a large event room used for formal parties and celebrations and includes tables and a wine-tasting bar. The upper level is large enough for 300 people (yes, it's a very big barn).

# *U*niquities:

- oldest winery in Maryland
- founded in 1945 by Philip Wagner, famous wine pioneer and author
- beautiful setting and great facilities

Boordy has a diverse selection of wines to choose from. Everyone should be able to find a wine to take home with them. Of the wines, the Boordy White and Red are the biggest sellers, while the Chardonnay and Cabernet Sauvignon are the most honored.

Half of the vineyards lie on site while the other half are located in Burkettsville, Maryland. The newest vineyard consists of Chardonnay grapes reserved for Boordy's champagne. When you visit, you'll drive between two vineyards: reds on the left and whites on the right. Take the time to investigate the grapes and check their progress.

Boordy's owners like to think their winery imparts "Maryland Sun, Soil and Soul" to their customers. Their wines are very reasonably priced and well-made, and the winery's setting is magnificent.

Make sure you take advantage of the tour, and say hello to the resident wine dogs—Owen, Allie and, Janus.

# Wine List

Sur Lie Reserve

Seyval Blanc

Chardonnay

Boordy White

White Riesling

Vidal Blanc

Boordy Blush

Apple White

Sweet Peach

Blanc de Blancs Sparkling Wine

Boordy Red

Cabernet Sauvignon

Wassail

Summer Spice

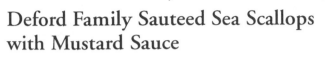

# *R*ecipes

## Deford Family Sauteed Sea Scallops with Mustard Sauce

3/4 lb sea scallops

1 large shallot, minced

2 tbsp Dijon mustard

2 tbsp cold unsalted butter, cut into bits

2 scallion greens, cut diagonally into 1/4 inch slices (about 2 tbsp)

1 1/2 tablespoons olive oil

1/4 cup water

1/4 cup Boordy Chardonnay

Remove tough muscle from side of each scallop if necessary. Pat scallops dry and season with salt and pepper. In a 10-12 inch non-stick skillet, heat oil over moderately high heat until hot but not smoking and saute scallops 1 to 2 minutes on each side (depending on size), or until golden and just cooked through. Transfer scallops with tongs to a plate and keep warm, covered loosely.

In oil remaining in skillet, cook shallot over moderate heat, stirring until softened. Add Boordy Chardonnay and boil for 1 minute, scraping up brown bits. Stir in water and mustard and simmer until reduced to about 1/4 cup. Add butter and swirl skillet, returning skillet to heat as necessary, until butter is just incorporated into sauce. Season sauce with salt and pepper.

Spoon sauce into a small platter or 2 plates. Top sauce with scallops and sprinkle with scallion.

*(This recipe was submitted by the Deford family of Boordy Vineyards.)*

MARYLAND 1995
OAK FERMENTED

PRODUCED AND BOTTLED BY CATOCTIN VINEYARDS, INC.
NEW HAMPSHIRE AVENUE AND GREENBRIDGE ROAD

# CATOCTIN VINEYARDS

| | |
|---|---|
| Founded: | 1983 |
| Owners: | Bob Lyon & Shahin Bagheri, Ann and Jerry Milne |
| Winemaker: | Bob Lyon |
| Address: | 805 Greenbridge Road Brookeville, MD 20833 |
| Phone: | (301) 774-2310 |
| Hours: | Saturdays and Sundays 12-5 p.m., Monday thru Friday by appointment only. Tastings, which include a souvenir glass, are $3.00. Large groups should call ahead. |
| Annual production: | 10,000 gallons |
| Price range of wines: | $6.00 to $11.00 (cellar selections, like the 1983 Cab can be $50) |
| Amenities available: | Bathrooms and 44 acres of picnic area. |
| Area Wineries: | Elk Run Vineyards and Winery Linganore Winecellars at Berrywine Plantation Loew Vineyards |
| Local attractions: | Washington, D.C. Patuxent River State Park Olney Theatre / Ale House |

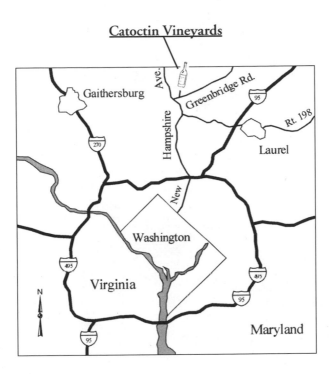

**Catoctin Vineyards**

## Directions:

From Washington: Go north on New Hampshire Avenue, crossing Route 108. Turn right on Greenbridge Road (you'll see a sign for the winery just before the turn). Make a left into the property, veering right on a gravel road. Drive slowly and be careful especially if it's wet. The winery is on the right.

From Baltimore: Take I-95 south to Route 32 north to Route 108. Go left (west) to Route 650 (New Hampshire Avenue) and go north four miles to Greenbridge Road. Turn right on Greenbridge Road (you'll see a sign for the winery just before the turn). Make a left into the property, veering right on a gravel road. Drive slowly and be careful especially if it's wet. The winery is on the right.

Catoctin Winery is tucked away in Montgomery County and is

rather isolated from the shuffle of Washington, surprisingly just 12 miles away. Set on beautiful grounds, the winery is surrounded by tall trees and a lake that lies just meters away. The winery is two stories and resembles an old Tudor building.

Bob Lyon, winemaker and co-owner, toils inside ensuring that all's well

*Catoctin's Bob Lyon pumps Cabernet Sauvignon into a fermentation tank.* with his award-
winning wines. He earned an enology degree from the University of California at Davis while spending evenings working at the Inglenook and Sebastiani wineries in the Sonoma and Napa Valleys.

Lyon was twenty-one when he started reading books about wine, but it took him twenty years to save up enough money to finally go to school and study winemaking. But, with his degree in hand, he spent a year performing his assistantship at Chateau Montelena in Napa where he says he really learned the process and art of wine-making.

Shortly after, Lyon and his partner Shahin moved to Maryland. He says he wanted to pioneer quality winemaking in the Mid-Atlantic. In 1979, he began working as winemaker with the now closed Byrd Vineyards in Myersville, Maryland, and was responsible for producing some of Byrd's highly acclaimed Chardonnays and Cabernets. Lyon left Byrd Vineyards in 1983 after purchasing the old Provenza Winery for his own winery. He formed a partnership with the Milnes who had already established a vineyard in the Catoctin Mountains.

The name Catoctin comes from Native Americans and means "where the deer roam." Lyon chose the name after selecting a vineyard site nestled in the hills of Maryland's Catoctin Mountains. He says the soil of the Catoctin—which is rich in minerals—makes the wine "seriously complex," a trait found in many of his wines. Catoctin has about thirty acres of vines in production consisting of Chardonnay, Cabernet Sauvignon, Seyval and Cabernet Franc.

Catoctin's Eye of the Oriole is the winery's best seller. It's a pleasant blush with a name that brings in the fans. Lyon's other wines speak of his winemaking experience. He says Catoctin bears some of the finest table wines on the East Coast. Lyon has cellared a few cases of each of his releases since 1983 and occasionally gives tastings of his new wines in comparison to his old: an interesting olfactory history of his wines.

# Uniquities:

- California-trained winemaker, Bob Lyon
- closest winery to D.C.
- Lyon keeps a library of his wines from years past

Catoctin partner Anne Milne says the wine greatly complements food. If she had her way, there would be a restaurant at the winery to facilitate the matchmaking of wine and food. "If the winery wasn't so far removed, the restaurant would have been here a long time ago," says Milne. Restaurant or not, this winery is worth the visit.

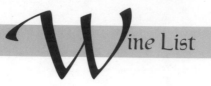

# Wine List

Chardonnay

Chardonnay — oak fermented

Cabernet Sauvignon

Cabernet Franc

Johannisberg Riesling

Eye of the Beholder

Eye of the Oriole

Mariage

Apple Dew

Persian Apple (peach)

# ecipes

## Ann's Riesling Zabaglione:

**Cake:**
One half-sheet vanilla cake (11 x 17 inches)

**Pears:**

| | |
|---|---|
| 12 ripe firm pears | 2 1/4 cups granulated sugar |
| 1 1/2 cup Catoctin Riesling | 3 tbsp fresh lemon juice |

Peel and core pears, and slice them 1/2 inches thick. Combine all ingredients in large saute pan. Cook over medium heat until pears are cooked but still slightly firm to the touch; they must hold their shape. Remove pears with slotted spoon and drain; reserve cooking liquid.

**Riesling Zabaglione:**

| | |
|---|---|
| 12 large egg yolks | 3/4 cup granulated sugar |
| 1 1/8 cup Catoctin Riesling | 2 cups heavy whipping cream |
| pinch of salt | |

Fill a medium saucepan less than half full of water, and bring to a slow boil. In a stainless bowl, whisk together all but the whipping cream. Set bowl over hot water, ensuring that the bottom of the bowl does not touch water, and whisk constantly until mixture is thick. Immediately set bowl into a larger bowl filled with water and ice cubes, and whisk until mixture is cool.

In a separate bowl, whip the cream until soft peaks are formed. Fold into egg mixture.

**Assembly:**
1 oz square of bittersweet chocolate

Cut cake in half lengthwise. Using 2 1/2 quart glass trifle bowl, make dents in cake with bowl rim to form circles and partial circles. Cut within these marks to make circles to fit inside trifle bowl. Use edges and leftover pieces to fill in the partial circles during the assembly.

Put 1/4 cup sabayon mix in trifle bowl to cover bottom. Fit a cake round over this. Using a pastry brush, paint the surface of the round with the reserved pear cooking liquid. Arrange pear slices, slightly overlapped, in circles on cake round, beginning with outer ring touching bowl. When completed, cover this with 1 cup sabayon mix. Continue in this way until all cake and pears are used, finishing the trifle with a layer of sabayon. Shave bittersweet chocolate curls over top of sabayon with a vegetable peeler.

Refrigerate for at least six hours before serving. Serve with small glasses of Catoctin Johannisberg Riesling.

*(This recipe was submitted by Ann Milne of Catoctin Winery.)*

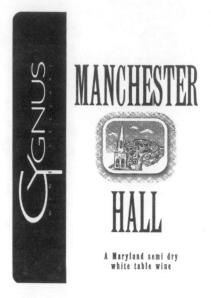

A Maryland semi dry
white table wine

# CYGNUS WINE CELLARS

| | |
|---|---|
| Founded: | 1996 |
| Owners: | Ray Brasfield |
| Winemaker: | Ray Brasfield |
| Address: | 3130 Long Lane |
| | Manchester, MD 21102 |
| Phone: | (410) 374-6395 |
| Hours: | Saturdays and Sundays 12-5 p.m., other times by appointment only. Tastings and tours are free. |
| Annual production: | 2,500 gallons |
| Price range of wines: | $9.00 to $12.00 |
| Amenities available: | Bathroom, winery are fully handicapped accessible. Picnic area behind the winery and covered area in front of the winery. |
| Area Wineries: | Elk Run Vineyards and Winery |
| | Loew Vineyards |
| Local attractions: | Historic city of Manchester |
| | Antique shops in town |
| | Carroll County Farm Museum |
| | Gettysburg |

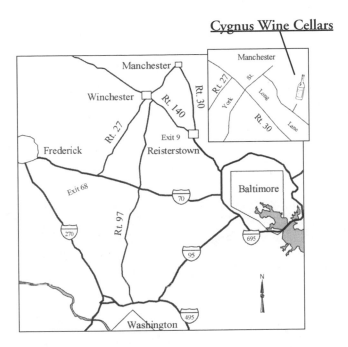

## Directions:

From Washington: Take I-495 to Route 97 north to Westminster. Turn left onto Route 140. Exit onto Route 27 north. At Manchester, turn right (south) onto Rt. 30 (Main Street) and go two blocks to traffic light. Turn left onto York Street, then right onto Long Lane and look for the white winery building and Cygnus sign on the left.

From Baltimore: Take I-695 to I-795 north. Take exit 9 (Route 30) to Manchester. Turn right at Beaver Street, left onto Long Lane and follow two blocks to winery on the right and look for the white winery building and Cygnus sign on the left.

Cygnus is one of Maryland's newest wineries. Located just one block off Main Street in historic Manchester in Carroll County, Cygnus is in a unique spot for a winery. Even more unique is the 60-year-old building where the winery is located. If you look closely overhead at the ceiling, you can see the racks used in the building's former life as a slaughter house.

"It works perfectly as a winery," says Brasfield, as he shows off the many amenities the former slaughterhouse provides. In the back there is a freezer room where he stores the wine after it is bottled. In the basement, oak barrels are stacked just outside another freezer room where he keeps his champagne where it is bottle-fermented.

*Ray Brasfield poses with his wines at the Maryland Wine Festival.*

Brasfield buys his grapes from Maryland and Pennsylvania vineyards, allowing him to select only the best fruit. He crushes the grapes and ferments all the wine on site, using the built-in lab to monitor sugar and Ph levels throughout the process.

Brasfield is no stranger to winemaking. He made his first wine in 1981 at home in Baltimore. Brasfield and his wife moved to Maryland in 1978 and leased the winery building in 1996. He is

also the wine consultant at Woodhall Vineyards and Wine Cellars in Parkton, Maryland. Ray is very knowledgeable on the topic of winemaking and is the man to answer all of your questions while touring the winery or in the tasting room.

The entrance to the winery can be recognized by the large sliding barn doors. The bar inside is constructed using old slats from the same barn from which the front doors came. The tasting room is spacious and airy, while still retaining the austere atmosphere of a slaughter house.

# Uniquities:

- most unique location— in an old slaughterhouse
- located in downtown historic Manchester
- winemaker Brasfield makes a great champagne

When trying the wines, notice the names on the labels. Manchester Hall is a semidry white table wine named for the staff of the Town Hall of Manchester. Brasfield's Millers Time is a fun wine with a familiar name. From there, the names may be ordinary, but the wines are exceptional.

Take the Cygnus Red, for example. It is a fresh wine—not too complex, but it has enough body to match the flavors of grilled and roasted meats. The Cygnus Chardonnay is also a wonderful wine. "It's really elegant," says Brasfield, describing how well it goes with fish and other seafood.

When talking with Brasfield, you will come to realize how intertwined he is with the town of Manchester. He is always a key player in "Manchester Day" celebrations and says that the town has been supportive of him and his winery from the beginning.

Cygnus Winery is one of a kind and its setting in Manchester make it a nice day trip. Enjoy the historic town and the surrounding antique shops, and leave room in the trunk for some wine.

# Wine List

Cygnus Red

Cygnus White

Manchester Hall

Millers Time

Cabernet Sauvignon

Royele, classic method sparkling wine

Port of Manchester

# *R*ecipes

## Muphen's Basil-Parmesan Popovers

Shortening or non-stick cooking spray to coat 6 custard cups,
muffin tins, or popover pan

2 eggs, beaten                           1 cup milk
1 tbsp cooking oil                       1 cup all-purpose flour
2 tsp dried, crushed basil leaves        1 tsp salt
2 tbsp grated fresh Parmesan cheese

Preheat oven to 400 degrees.  Coat cups or muffin tin with shortening or cooking spray.  Place the cups or muffin tin on a 15x10x1 inch
baking pan and set aside.  In a mixing bowl combine: eggs, milk, and
cooking oil.  Add flour, salt, basil, and Parmesan cheese.  Whisk
until smooth.  Fill the greased cups full.  Bake in the preheated 400
degree oven about 40 minutes, or until very firm.  Prick each popover
with a fork immediately after removing from oven to allow the steam
to escape.  If crisper popovers are desired: turn off the oven and return
the popovers to the oven for 5 to 10 minutes or until the desired crispness is reached.  Serve hot!  Serves 6.  Serve with Cygnus Red.

## World's Easiest, Tastiest Chicken

1 cup each lemon juice & orange juice        2 tbsp vegetable oil
6 cloves garlic, crushed or finely chopped    Salt and pepper to taste
1 tsp each ground ginger and crushed tarragon leaves
6 pieces boneless, skinless chicken breast

Combine all ingredients except chicken in a large bowl or baking dish.
Add chicken and cover.  Marinate in refrigerator at least 2 hours (can
be marinated up to 8 hours).  Drain chicken.  Discard all but 2 tbsp
of marinade.  Grill, bake, or broil chicken (using reserved marinade)
until chicken is fully cooked.  Serves 4-6.  Serve with Cygnus White.

*(These recipes were submitted by Muphen Whitney,
Communications Director for the Association of Maryland Wineries.)*

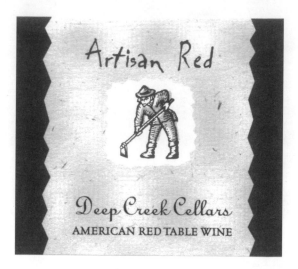

# DEEP CREEK CELLARS

| | |
|---|---|
| Founded: | 1997 |
| Owners: | Paul Roberts and Nadine Grabania |
| Winemaker: | Paul Roberts |
| Address: | 177 Frazee Ridge Road |
| | Friendsville, MD 21531 |
| Phone: | (301) 746-4349 |
| Hours: | Summer, Fridays after 3 p.m., Saturdays 11 a.m. to 7 p.m.  Other times by appointment.  Closed January through March and major holidays.  (More regular sales hours are planned by mid-1999.  Please call.)  Tastings and tours are free. |
| Annual production: | 2,500 gallons |
| Price range of wines: | $6.70 to $11.00 |
| Amenities available: | Bathrooms, picnic areas |
| Local attractions: | Deep Creek Lake |
| | Numerous bed and breakfasts |
| | Frank Lloyd Wright's "Fallingwater" |
| | Ohiopyle (PA) State Park |

## Deep Creek Cellars

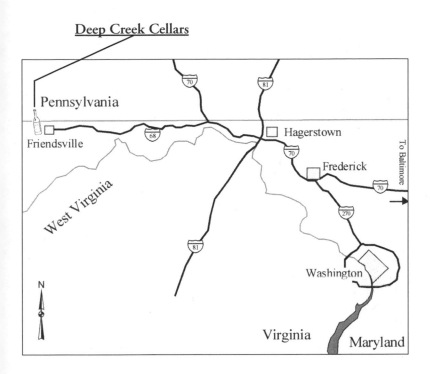

### Directions:

From Washington: Take I-270 north to I-70 west. Take I-68 west to Friendsville (exit 4) and go north on Route 42 six miles. Turn right on Frazee Ridge Road (just after the big red barn); the winery is on the left halfway up the hill.

From Baltimore: Take I-70 west to I-68 west. Continue to Friendsville (exit 4) and go north on Route 42 six miles. Turn right on Frazee Ridge Road (just after the big red barn); the winery is on the left halfway up the hill.

Just minutes from Deep Creek Lake lies the Maryland wine industry's greatest secret: Deep Creek Cellars. Owners Paul Roberts and Nadine Grabania have built their winery in one of the most beautiful regions in the state. At 2,100 feet, the winery sits atop a south-facing hill in the midst of farmland. You can hear the nearby cows and horses and perhaps the sputter of a tractor as you enter the winery.

Once inside, you get an immediate feel for this husband and wife team. The walls are lined with racks of wine and artwork by Nadine and friends.

There is no tasting bar: there is only a table. Paul, a humble man with an unequalled smile, welcomes you in and invites you to sit down for a taste of his wines.

Paul is the primary winemaker, but Nadine puts in equally long hours. "We tend the vineyard together, make wine together, bottle and sell wine together," says Paul. "Family and friends help out, too!" Both Paul and Nadine hold positions with museums in Pittsburgh where

*Winemaker Paul Roberts poses in-front of his young vineyard.*

they currently reside but have plans to relocate to their winery in the near future.

"My friends think I'm nuts," says Nadine describing her dual life as a Pittsburgh professional and winery owner. She is also a wonderful painter starving for more time to do what she loves. Nadine says relocating to Friendsville will allow her and Paul more time to be creative.

Paul is working on a book of meditations on wine growing. He hopes to publish soon, so make sure you ask about the book's progress when you visit.

The winery is built into the hillside and will eventually become the foundation for Paul and Nadine's house. But for now, it serves its purpose well as the winery and tasting room. The fermenting wine can be seen racked behind the double sliding doors.

"Everything is lightly oaked and unfiltered," which Paul says preserves the wine's fruit flavors. "Just leave the bottle upright for a few minutes before serving to allow the sediment to settle," he tells some customers.

### Uniquities:
- newest winery in Maryland
- best valued wines (and they are wonderful!)
- great day or weekend getaway, right next to Deep Creek Lake!

The wine at Deep Creek Cellars is very well made. And it's inexpensive, too! When you pay $6.70 for Paul's Artisan Red table wine you're really getting what could very well be confused with a more expensive southern French country wine. It's a deep red wine made from Carignan, Grenache, and native Cynthiana grapes that will go with just about any food. The white is citrusy and soft—"a shellfish wine," says Paul.

Paul and Nadine are currently pouring Artisan Red and White and Watershed Red Reserve with plans to produce a sweet fruit wine and a fruit/grape blended wine. Once their vineyards are ready, look for Cabernet Franc and Chardonnay, too.

Paul spent a year at Chateau Montelena in California as an apprentice where he learned the skills he employs at Deep Creek Cellars. He's taken this knowledge and is realizing his dreams while making his wonderful wines accessible to everyone. Deep Creek Cellars certainly lives up to its slogan: "Local wines . . . faraway flavors."

# ine List

Artisan White

Artisan Red

Watershed Red Reserve

# *R*ecipes

## Whole Grain and Tomato Casserole

Combine two modest handfuls of bulgar wheat, steel-cut oats, or pearled barley with fresh chopped kale, spinach, or chard and un-cooked penne regatta, fusili, or other small rolled pasta in a baking dish. Season lightly with salt and pepper, garlic, balamic vinegar, wine, a smidge of molasses or honey, and savory pan-Mediterranean spices like sumac, cardomom, allspice. Dice in 3 or 4 medium summer tomatoes, or the equivalent in canned tomatoes and juice—unripe or unflavorful tomatoes kill this recipe—and two big dollups of cottage or ricotta cheese. If you want, add a little chopped pancetta, prosciutto, anchovy, or even lean bacon. (Cook bacon first and remove from grease). Combine. Add some water or more wine, if need be, to make enough juice in the dish to cook the pasta. Check during baking, too.

Bake covered at 350 degrees for about 50 minutes or until pasta is al dente. Garnish with fresh Italian herbs like oregano, basil, and thyme, and serve the Artisan Red slightly chilled. Serves 2.

## Butternut Burritos

Half a butternut or acorn squash and bake face down in a covered dish at 325 degrees for about 1 hour, until the squash flesh is soft. Prepare steamed rice. When the squash flesh is spooned out of its rind, it should have the consistency of refried beans. (You can make half-and-half squash and beans.) Add salt and pepper and shots of hot sauce. Whip a few strokes with a fork. Warm the burrito or taco shells. Serve the squash instead of ground meat as a filling with diced tomatoes, coarsely grated cheese; red onions, sunflower seeds, cilantro, and anything else you desire Tex Mex-wise. Rice on the side. The exotic squash filling marries so sweetly with the spicy blackberryness of Artisan Red, especially chilled.

*(In the style of Paul and Nadine's favorite cookbook, from Italy's Abruzzi, they avoid precise measures. Experiment. Improvise. Approximate. Substitute. Leave room for creativity.)*

.1997.
Pinot Noir
Maryland

TABLE WINE PRODUCED AND BOTTLED BY
ELK RUN VINEYARDS, MOUNT AIRY, MD  BWMD-30

# ELK RUN VINEYARDS and WINERY

| | |
|---|---|
| Founded: | 1983 |
| Owners: | Fred and Carol Wilson |
| Winemaker: | Fred Wilson |
| Address: | 15113 Liberty Road |
| | Mt. Airy, MD 21771 |
| Phone: | (410) 775-2513 |
| E-mail: | elk_run@msn.com |
| WWW: | www.elkrun.com |
| Hours: | Wednesday-Saturday 10-5 p.m., Sunday |
| | 1-5p.m., or by appointment.  Tastings |
| | and tours are free. Larger groups should call |
| | ahead and a small fee will be charged. |
| Annual production: | 10,000 gallons |
| Price range of wines: | $6.99 to $35.00 |
| Amenities available: | Picnic areas, bathrooms, warming kitchen |
| | for catering and seating for about 30 people. |
| Area Wineries: | Loew Vineyards (1.5 miles west on Route 26) |
| | Linganore Winecellars (directions at winery) |
| Local attractions: | New Market town and antiques shops |
| | Historic Frederick |
| | Carroll County Farm Museum |

## Elk Run Vineyards and Winery

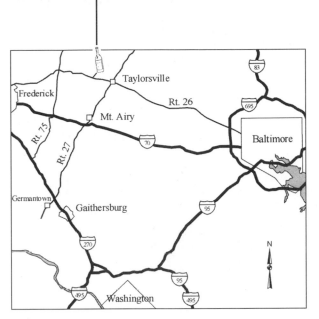

## Directions:

From Washington: Take I-270 to Father Hurley Boulevard. Turn right onto Route 27 north. Proceed through Mt. Airy to Taylorsville. Turn left on Route 26 and go 2.5 miles to the winery. Look for the big Elk Run and grape sign.

From Baltimore: Take I-70 to Mt. Airy. Turn right onto Route 27 north, proceeding 8 miles to Taylorsville. Turn left onto Route 26 and follow 2.5 miles to the winery. Look for the big Elk Run and grape sign.

Fred and Carol Wilson of Elk Run probably won't be the first to greet you at the winery. Champagne Billy, their friendly cocker spaniel, will most likely play the part of welcoming committee, leading you straight into the tasting room. The tasting room is actually the refurbished original winery building that looks over the vineyard through a large sliding glass door.

Inside, Carol conducts tastings for visitors at a long, spacious bar. With more than ten wines to try at any given time, it's best to make yourself at home and discover your favorites.

The house you pass on the way up the drive has been there since 1756 and is a county historical site. Tours are available during the summer. The owner of the house owned 700 acres in the area, and the land was legally titled "Cold Friday."

A stained-glass window marks the outer wall of the tasting room, while the new winery is guarded by an old arched church door.

*Elk Run's namesake watching over the CAVE.*

Both are from St. John's Church in Westminster. About ten feet high, the door conceals the CAVE, the winery and cellars where Elk Run's award-winning wines are produced and aged.

The vineyard to the left of the tasting room began in the basement of partner Neill Bassford in 1980. Now, those same Chardonnay, Cabernet Sauvignon, and Riesling vines (with Fred's help, of course) are producing outstanding wine. A new vineyard just across Route 26 was christened Cold Friday in 1995. Planted there are Cabernet Sauvignon, Cabernet Franc, Merlot, Chardonnay, and Pinot Noir grapes.

The secret to the great wines lies not only in the grapes, but in the care of the vineyards. "If you grow the best grapes in the best environment under the best conditions, you'll get a superior wine," claims Carol Wilson. Plus, she thinks Fred's palate is the key to consistently good wines year to year.

In 1991, Elk Run took over management of Mowbray vineyards, a successful winery of Maryland's past, owned and operated by Dr. Hamilton Mowbray. Today, Fred tends to the vineyards and from its harvest makes "Dr. Hamilton Mowbray Cabernet," a robust wine that tastes of history: the vines are some of the oldest on the east coast.

*U*niquities:
- wines are distributed internationally
- historic attributes of property (house dating from 1756)
- Only Maryland winery making Pinot Noir

This is just one of the excellent wines Wilson makes. A brut champagne made from Pinot Noir and Chardonnay is available (ask to see the champagne cellar hidden behind the two doors on the right of the tasting room) as well as a very sweet ice wine made from late-harvest Gewürtzraminer grapes called Vin de Jus Glacé (which won the 1997 and 1998 Governor's Cup Award).

The Wilsons have brought Elk Run a long way since it was first licensed in 1979. "We're expanding all the time," says Carol as she pours a glass of Pinot Noir, a variety being expanded in the vineyards.

For Elk Run, export is the name of the game. Their Johannisberg Riesling has been exported to Canada, while their Chardonnay and Sweet Katherine have made it all the way to London. Although it's not necessary to show your passport upon entry, it is always a good idea to bring luggage big enough for all your wine.

# 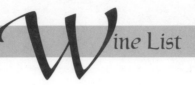ine List

Champagne

Sauvignon Blanc

Chardonnay

Liberty Tavern Chardonnay

Chesapeake Bay Sunset

Gewürztraminer

Johannisberg Riesling

Annapolis Sunset

Maryland Cabernet Sauvignon

Liberty Tavern Cabernet Sauvignon

Syrah

Dr. Mowbray Cabernet Sauvignon

Sweet Katherine

Vin de Jus Glace

# *R*ecipes

## Carol's Roast Lamb with Shiitake, Chocolate and Cabernet Sauvignon Gravy

| | |
|---|---|
| 1 leg of lamb | shiitake mushrooms |
| 2 cloves of garlic | currant jam |
| rosemary sprigs | butter |
| thyme sprigs | walnut oil |
| shallots | Cabernet Sauvignon |
| honey mustard | |

Cut the fat off the lamb, make slits and stuff with slices of garlic and herbs. Make a rub of honey mustard, currant jam, and herbs de Province and spread over the roast. Lay shallots on top of the roast.

Bake at 325° for 18-20 minutes to the pound with an internal temperature of 140 degrees until slightly pink.

Sauté shiitake mushrooms in 2 tablespoons of butter and a teaspoon of walnut oil. Add pan drippings and shallots, 2 cups of Cabernet Sauvignon, and one can of beef stock.

Simmer and reduce to 1/2 cup. Add 1/2 square of bitter chocolate. Slice lamb and pour gravy over.

## Elk Run Sangria

4 parts Sweet Katherine
1 part orange juice
2 parts tonic water
add sliced orange or lime
chill

*(This recipe was submitted by Carol Wilson of Elk Run Vineyards and Winery.)*

MARYLAND

## *Chambourcin*

DRY RED WINE

# FIORE WINERY

| | |
|---|---|
| Founded: | 1986 |
| Owners: | Mike, Rose and Eric Fiore |
| Wine makers: | Mike and Eric Fiore |
| Address: | 3026 Whiteford Road |
| | Pylesville, MD 21132 |
| Phone: | (410) 836-7605 |
| WWW: | http://FioreWinery.com |
| Hours: | Wednesday-Sunday 12-5 p.m. or by |
| | appointment. Tastings and tours are free. |
| | Advance notice and a small fee are requested |
| | for large groups. Closed major holidays. |
| Annual production: | 17,000 gallons |
| Price range of wines: | $6.00 to $19.50 |
| Amenities available: | Spacious rooms for events, bathrooms, |
| | picnic area and a boccie-ball court. |
| Area Wineries: | *"Mason-Dixon Wine Trail"* Wineries |
| Local attractions: | Ladew Topiary Gardens |
| | Rocks State Park |
| | Havre de Grace |
| | Susquehanna National Wildlife Refuge |
| | Susquehanna State Park |

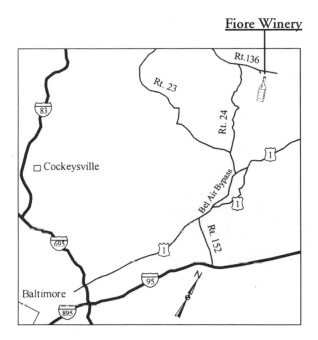

## Directions:

From Baltimore and Washington: Take I-95 north of I-695 to
exit 74 (Fallston). Proceed to the light and make a left onto
Route 152. Follow 152 to U.S. Route 1 and make a right at the
light. Follow Route 1 north (take Bel Air bypass) to Route 24
north (Rocks State Park). Follow Route 24 north through
beautiful Rocks State Park to Route 136. Make a right onto
Route 136 and proceed approximately one mile; turn right into
the winery. Pass the Fiores' house on the right and park in the
lot just before the winery building.

After the long and shady drive on Route 136, the trees finally give way to the beautiful Fiore Winery and La Felicetta Vineyard.

The winery is set atop the second highest peak in Harford County at an elevation of 600 feet. From this perch, the view reveals a landscape of rolling hills and farmland surrounding the property. "La strada del vino rosso" is their motto: the road to the red wine. If ever there was a vineyard reminiscent of a small Italian winery, this is it.

This is no coincidence! Mike Fiore, often seen tending to the vineyard with sunglasses and a white rimmed hat, was

*The gorgeous view from Fiore Winery's veranda.*

born and raised in Italy in a family whose winemaking tradition is well known (Thomas Jefferson asked Mike's ancestor Philip Mazzei to help establish a vineyard in Virginia). Mike was only 17 when he became a certified cellar master in Italy. Soon after, he left home and hard times behind and came to America where he met Rose and the rest is history. Mike returned briefly to Italy—just long enough to receive an enology/viticulture degree from the University of Florence.

When he thinks of Italy, he likes to remember how it used to be. "When I was young, Italy was an ocean of grapes. Now it's an ocean of olive trees and condominiums," Mike says. Continuing his family's 400-year tradition of producing great wines (not condos), Fiore made Maryland his home and planted his first grapes in 1982. Since then, he has juggled his winemaking and full-time job with Baltimore Gas & Electric. But that has not kept him from the vineyards.

Now, there are ten acres on site with an additional fifty acres on Maryland's eastern shore. Mike hopes to have most of his white grapes grown on the shore reserving his La Felicetta Vineyard for the reds.

To get to the tasting room, you must walk down steps, crossing a footbridge to walk over a small stream while being surrounded by many different plants and flowers. There are plenty of opportunities to sit and enjoy the landscaping amongst the flowers or on the veranda of the tasting room, but there is a greater treat awaiting you inside.

Mike has extended the family tradition of winemaking to his son, Eric, who currently tends to the white wines allowing his father to concentrate on the reds. From Caronte, a deep blend of Cabernet Sauvignon and Sangiovese, to their light Blush of Bel Air, the Fiores produce many solid wines to suit a variety of tastes. Fiore's 1995 Chambourcin received a silver medal competing with 1,900 other wines at a recent Orange County, California, competition. Mike's next project is to produce a sparkling wine to be released "when the time is right."

# Uniquities:

- as Italian as is legal in Maryland (kidding, of course!)
- Most scenic winery setting
- Boccie-ball court is always open for games!

There is time for play amidst all the work—Mike will happily take a break, succumbing to any challenge to a boccie match. "One thing this winery has been missing all these years is a boccia court," Mike says. "Now, it's complete."

"A vineyard will only give you what you give it," says Mike, explaining why he works so hard. "The more work you put in it, the better product and quality you're going to have." At Fiore Winery, the truth is in the wines.

# Wine List

Cabernet Sauvignon

Chambourcin

Caronte (blend of vinifera reds)

Rosato

Chardonnay

Vidal Blanc

L'Ombra—venetian style of white wine

Vignoles

Scarlette

The Blush of Bel Air

Peach Floret (peach wine)

Gala White (apple wine)

## ecipes

## Rose's Chicken Cacciatore

1/4 cup butter
2 chickens (3 lbs each)
1 green pepper, thinly sliced
1 can (16 oz) Italian tomatoes
1 tsp brown sugar
few dashes of Worcestershire sauce
salt and freshly ground black pepper

1/4 cup olive oil
2 medium finely chopped onions
2-3 cloves of garlic, minced
1 tsp Italian seasoning
1/2 cup Fiore Rosato red wine

In a deep heavy skillet, heat the butter and oil and saute the chicken pieces until golden brown on all sides. Add onion, green pepper, and garlic and saute until soft. Season to taste with salt and pepper. Mix in the undrained tomatoes, Italian seasoning, and brown sugar. Bring to a boil, cover, and simmer over low heat for 30 minutes, stirring occasionally. Add wine and a few dashes of Worcestershire sauce. Simmer for another 15 minutes or until chicken is tender. Serves six.

## Figs in Wine & Honey

1 pound of fresh or dried figs
1/2 cup honey
pinch of cinnamon

Dry Fiore Vidal Blanc, to cover
1/2 tsp grated lemon peel
heavy cream

Place figs in a saucepan with wine to cover. Bring to a boil, then stir in honey, add grated lemon peel and cinnamon. Simmer uncovered, very gently until figs are tender. Cool, then chill. Serve with heavy cream. Serves four.

*(These recipes were submitted by the Fiore family.)*

# LINGANORE WINECELLARS
## at BERRYWINE PLANTATION

| | |
|---|---|
| Founded: | 1976 |
| Owners: | Jack and Lucille Aellen |
| Winemaker: | Anthony Aellen |
| Address: | 13601 Glissans Mill Road |
| | Mt. Airy, MD 21771 |
| Phone: | (410) 795-6432, (301) 831-5889 |
| WWW: | www.linganore-wine.com |
| Hours: | Weekdays 10-5 p.m., Saturday 10-6 p.m. and Sunday 12-6 p.m.  Closed major holidays (including Mother's, Father's and Independence Days).  Large groups should call ahead. |
| Annual production: | 55,000 gallons |
| Price range of wines: | $7.00 to $15.00 ($20.00 375 ml Sweet Chessie) |
| Amenities available: | Bathrooms, picnic areas. |
| Area Wineries: | Elk Run Vineyards and Winery |
| | Loew Vineyards |
| Local attractions: | New Market town and antiques shops |
| | Cunningham Falls State Park |
| | Historic Frederick |

## Linganore Winecellars

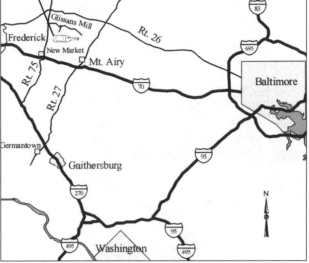

### Directions:

From Baltimore:   Take I-70 west to exit 62 New Market. Go north on Route 75 (4.5 miles).   Turn right just before the concrete bridge onto Glissans Mill Road.   Go 3.7 miles to the winery on your right.

From Washington:  Take I-270 north to Hyattstown exit (Route 109).  Turn left onto Route 109 and then left again onto Route 355.  Turn right onto Route 75 and follow for 13 miles.  Turn right just before the concrete bridge onto Glissans Mill Road.  Go 3.7 miles to the winery on your right.

Enjoy the beautiful valley through which Glissans Mill Road winds alongside a small, winding stream. This very green drive takes you to the arched-stone sign announcing your arrival at Linganore Winecellars. You drive between vineyards and see a lake on the left just before seeing the winery up the hill on the right. The whole setting has a casual feel that is reinforced upon entering the tasting room. Long-time friends. That's what the folks at Linganore make you feel like. And to top that, their wine gives you all the more reason to make yourself at home!

Linganore was founded in 1976 by Jack and Lucille Aellen who

have since put their two sons, Anthony and Eric, in charge of the winemaking and vineyards. They started with fruit wines but have since added dozens of wines to the list. Their wines have been a favorite in Maryland for many years, and they recently christened Chessie Racing in the Whitbread with

*Anthony and Eric Aellen stir a large vat of just-harvested grapes.*

a bottle of their 1996 Chessie's Legend.

You won't see any medals hanging in the tasting room. That doesn't mean Linganore is a stranger to awards. "Awards don't mean anything," says Anthony Aellen. "If you don't like it, who cares if it got an award?" Perhaps it's enough to know that Linganore is currently the largest winery in Maryland.

Take a seat at the wrap-around bar, or ask for a tour. Anthony tries to be available for tours and Lucille is usually in the tasting room—both are wealths of knowledge and laughter. (There's no need to take notes while Lucille tells you great recipes to go with

each wine...her recipe book is on sale in the store).

With thirty wines at any given time, the Aellens literally have something for everyone. Of these wines, about half are fruit wines and are bottled under the Berrywine Planta-tion label. These include Blueberry, Raspberry, Strawber-ry, Peach, and Plum. They range from super dry to semisweet and are built to be enjoyed with or without food (or dessert). Anthony gave me a blind tasting of his Dry Blueberry which I thought was a Mer-lot—a mistake made by everyone that day in the tasting room.

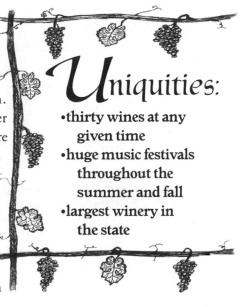

*U*niquities:
- **thirty wines at any given time**
- **huge music festivals throughout the summer and fall**
- **largest winery in the state**

Under the Linganore Winecellars label you'll find more than a dozen semidry to dry red and white table wines. Some, like the Chancellor and Cabernet Sauvignon, are classic wines. Most are easy-drinking wines that can be enjoyed with food or just sipped after a long day. Lucille introduces their Mt. White as "Welch's grape juice—with a kick."

The Aellens also make some unique wines found nowhere else in Maryland. They make a mead which is a traditional medieval drink made solely from fermented honey. Then there is the Tej, made with honey and a secret herb to complement spicy foods (it actually takes the burn out!). And don't be shy when it comes to the Dan-delion wine—it may be your only time to try it: Linganore claims to be the only commercial winery in the United States which makes it!

"It's neat to see where we've come from," Anthony says. Check in to see how far they've come over the years—and enjoy the wine! Be sure to find out about Linganore's music and wine festivals.

# Wine List

Chessie's Legend

White Raven

Terrapin White

Chancellor

Cabernet Sauvignon

Skipjack

Steeple Chase Red

Mt. White

Raspberry (both a dry & a sweet)

Blueberry (both a dry & a sweet)

Mead

Tej

Plum

Dandelion

# Recipes

## Lucille's Crab Casserole

| | |
|---|---|
| 1/2 lb package egg noodles | 3 tbsp butter |
| 3 tbsp flour | 3/4 tsp salt |
| 1/8 tsp pepper | 3 cups milk |
| 1/4 cup Linganore Terrapin White | 1 tbsp soy sauce |
| 3 1-oz cans crab meat (drained) | 1 tbsp A-1 Steak Sauce |
| 2 cups (1/2 lb) shredded cheddar cheese | 1/3 cup chopped pimento |
| 1 4-oz can sliced mushrooms (drained) | |
| 1/3 cup toasted, slivered almonds | |
| 1/3 cup shredded cheddar cheese | |

Cook noodles according to package directions: drain.  In saucepan, melt butter.

Blend flour, salt and pepper.  Remove from heat.  Gradually stir in milk, wine, soy sauce, and A-1 Steak Sauce.  Cook over medium heat, stirring constantly until thickened.

Cook 2 minutes longer.  In large bowl, combine crab meat, cheese, mushrooms, pimento, almonds.  Pour sauce all over ingredients. Sprinkle top with additional shredded cheese.

Bake in preheated oven at 350° F for 40-50 minutes.  Serves 8.

## Divinity Fondue

1 pkg of large marshmallows        1 pkg of milk chocolate fondue
1 bottle of a Berrywine fruit or Linganore Spicy Regatta wine

Marinate marshmallows in fruit wine for 1 hour.  Melt milk chocolate in fondue pot and keep very warm.  Dip each marshmallow in fondue and allow to melt a little.

*(These recipes were submitted by Lucille Aellen of Linganore Winecellars.)*

MARYLAND
# Honey & Grape
SWEET WINE
Alcohol 10.5% by volume

## LOEW VINEYARDS

| | |
|---|---|
| Founded: | 1982 |
| Owners: | Bill and Lois Loew |
| Winemaker: | Bill Loew |
| Address: | 14001 Liberty Road (Route 26) |
| | Mt. Airy, MD 21771 |
| Phone: | (301) 831-5464 |
| Hours: | Saturdays 10-5 p.m. and Sunday 1-5 p.m. |
| | Weekdays by appointment. Closed major |
| | holidays. Large groups should call ahead. |
| | Tours and tastings are free. |
| Annual production: | 3,000 gallons |
| Price range of wines: | $7.50 to $15.00 |
| Amenities available: | Bathrooms, picnic areas |
| Area Wineries: | Elk Run Vineyards and Winery |
| | Linganore Winecellars at Berrywine Plantation |
| Local attractions: | New Market town and antiques shops |
| | Catoctin Mountain Recreation Area |
| | Cunningham Falls State Park |
| | Historic Frederick |
| | Carroll County Farm Museum |

Loew Vineyards

## Directions:

From Washington: Take I-270 to Father Hurley Boulevard. Turn right on Route 27 north. Proceed through Mt. Airy to Taylorsville. Turn left onto Route 26 going west and drive five miles to the winery. Look for the Loew Vineyards sign in a field on the left just 100 yards before the winery, which is also on the left.

From Baltimore: Take I-70 to Mt. Airy. Turn right on Route 27 north, proceeding eight miles to Taylorsville. Turn left onto Route 26 going west and drive five miles to the winery. Look for the Loew Vineyards sign in a field on the left just 100 yards before the winery, which is also on the left.

As you make your way up the driveway, you'll see the Loew house on the left and the winery building straight ahead. The pine trees on the left hide the vineyard from unsuspecting visitors, but you will find it a treat to take a tour with winemaker Bill Loew, who walks his guests through the process of grape-growing.

You can count on meeting Lois Loew in the tasting room: she is the tasting room staff. Immediately, you will realize that this is one of the smallest and most personal of Maryland's wineries. It's so easy to strike up a conversation with Bill and Lois and so rewarding too.

Lois holds a full-time position as a psychologist with Montgomery County Schools and is at the winery every open hour. Bill works full time at the winery and enjoys making unique wines. After all, he has a reputation to live up to: his family began making wine in the 1800s in the Austro-Hungarian empire through the 1930s and when you try his wine, you'll taste that tradition.

The tasting room and the entire wine-making operation are housed in a small unassuming building nestled into a hill. The tasting room comes complete with a photo-tour on the back wall showing the entire grape-growing process. You will probably be

*Bill Loew and friend Herb Kirch dump grapes in the crusher.*

greeted by Higgins, the friendly wine cat, whose main job is to supervise the tasting room operation. The Loews have all sorts of wine paraphernalia as well as apparel for sale (don't forget about the wine).

"I have filled every bottle we've sold," says Bill, very proud of the hands-on approach of his small winery. He says his goal is to make very different wines from everyone else's. "And we're having a lot of fun doing it," adds Lois as she and Bill give a tour of the winery, located just behind the tasting room. Here is where Bill ferments and ages his many wines.

Of their 37 acres of land, only 5.5 acres are planted with grapes. "This is enough for one family to handle," says Bill looking over his vineyard from atop the hillside. The hill is planted with vinifera and French hybrid grapes. If you tour the vineyard, you'll walk through nine varieties of grapes: Chardonnay, Cabernet Sauvignon,

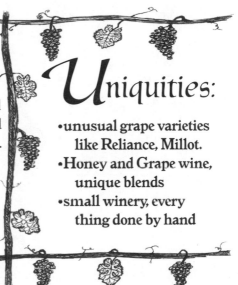

*U*niquities:

- unusual grape varieties like Reliance, Millot.
- Honey and Grape wine, unique blends
- small winery, every thing done by hand

Cabernet Franc, Seyval, Millot, Chancellor, Foch, Reliance, and Riesling. The vineyard began as a one-acre planting in 1982.

From their grapes, the Loews make ten to thirteen wines every year. Twilight, Honey and Grape, and Serendipity are some of their more distinctive wines. Twilight wine is a blend of Riesling and Seyval yielding a semisweet wine. Their Honey and Grape wine is made with barrel-fermented honey and Seyval. It's semisweet and is suited for immediate consumption or a few years of cellaring. The Reliance French-hybrid grape is a nice seedless eating grape, but Bill tried making a wine out of it. "It was such a pleasant surprise, we called it Serendipity."

Take advantage of the opportunity to talk and taste with Bill and Lois—and enjoy your time spent with them.

# Wine List

Chardonnay

Chardonnay in Pink

Harvest Gold

Honey & Grape

Apples and Honey

Twilight

Celebration

Johannisberg Riesling

Serendipity

Cabernet Sauvignon

Harvest Red

Classic Red

Blueberry

# Recipes

## Loew's Chicken Round-Up

3 lbs chicken parts                salt and pepper to taste
1 large onion, sliced              3 cloves garlic, chopped
1 tsp oregano                      1 tsp marjoram
1/2 cup sliced carrots             1/2 cup chopped celery
1 can stewed tomatoes             1 1/2 cups chicken broth
1/2 cup Harvest Red wine

Brown chicken in large pot.  Push chicken to the side, and saute the onions and garlic lightly.  Add remaining ingredients.  Cover and simmer for 30 to 45 minutes, or until chicken is tender.  Add liquid as required.  Serve over rice, wild rice or pasta.

## Giorgio's Crab Sauce

3 lbs fresh chopped plum tomatoes, (blanched with skins and seeds removed)
1/2 cup extra virgin olive oil          1/2 cup of Loew Chardonnay
4 large cloves of fresh minced garlic          1 small white onion diced
1 carrot, peeled and diced
1 lb backfin crab meat (and 4-6 left-over crabs if available)
2 tbsp fresh chopped Italian (flat-leaf) parsley
1 lb linguini (or pasta of your choice)
salt, fresh ground pepper, and Old Bay seasoning to taste

In a large saute pan/skillet, add the oil, carrot, and onion.  Cook on a medium low flame until the onions soften and turn translucent.  Add the garlic and wine and continue cooking for 2-3 minutes or until the wine is reduced.  Add the tomatoes and cook over medium heat for about 15 minutes.  Add the salt, pepper, and Old Bay to taste. (This should be a rather spicy sauce.)  Add crabs/crab meat and cook sauce for another 10 minutes.  Add the parsley about two minutes before you plate this dish.  Pasta should be cooked very "al dente."  Please note: In Italy, one never serves grated cheese as an accompaniment with seafood, and I suggest doing without - but if you can't live without the grated cheese - use Romano - it will have more of a bite than Parmigiana.

*(The first recipe was submitted by Lois Loew of Loew Vineyards.*
*The second recipe was submitted by George Miller, director of the Liturgy and Music at Loyola College.)*

# WOODHALL VINEYARDS and WINE CELLARS

| | |
|---|---|
| Founded: | 1983 |
| Owners: | Al Copp, Chris and Pat Lang |
| Winemaker: | Al Copp; Ray Brasfield, wine consultant; Chris Kent, cellar master |
| Address: | 17912 York Road Parkton, MD 21120 |
| Phone: | (410) 357-8644 |
| Hours: | Tuesday through Sunday 12 p.m.-5 p.m. Closed major holidays. Tours and tastings are free. Large groups are charged a nominal fee and should call ahead. |
| Annual production: | 6,000 gallons |
| Price range of wines: | $7.00 to $25.00 |
| Amenities available: | Bathrooms, picnic area, adjacent trout stream |
| Area Wineries: | *"Mason-Dixon Wine Trail"* Wineries Basignani Winery |
| Local attractions: | Gunpowder Falls State Park NCR Hike and Bike Trail Oregon Ridge |

## Woodhall Vineyards and Wine Cellars

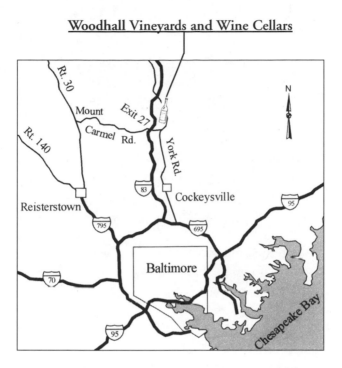

### Directions:

From Washington: Take I-95 north to 695 (Baltimore beltway) heading toward Towson. Take I-83 north to Mt. Carmel Road (exit 27) east to York Road. Go north 1.8 miles to Woodhall which is on the left just past the Gunpowder River.

From Baltimore: Take I-83 north to Mt. Carmel Road (exit 27) east to York Road. Go north 1.8 miles to Woodhall which is on the left just past the Gunpowder River.

Just a few minutes off I-83, Woodhall provides a respite for travelers between Baltimore and Harrisburg. Of course, the folks at the winery welcome everyone for a visit and have enough wines to go around.

When you turn into the driveway, notice the young vines planted on the hill to the right. These are Chardonnay, Merlot, Cabernet Franc, and Chambourcin grapes. While most of the grapes used by Woodhall come from vineyards in Maryland, including their own, others come from growers outside the state.

"We use only the best grapes," says Al Copp to a customer while pouring wine at the Maryland Wine Festival in Carroll County. Copp says Woodhall strives to be one of the premier wineries on the East Coast producing only serious, high-quality wines. So far so good.

Even amidst all this seriousness, Copp is jovial and very interested in what customers think of Woodhall's products. He asks everyone their thoughts and seems to take mental notes from their responses.

Woodhall produces a good variety of wines that fall into three categories: everyday table wines, premium wines, and more complex

*Woodhall's Al Copp pours wine at the Maryland Wine Festival.*

varietals. All are well-made, and tasting through them allows customers to try a mix of styles and complexities.

All but one of the wines are blends of grapes from different locations ensuring only the best fruit is used. The Reserve Cabernet Sauvignon from Copernica Vineyards is the exception to the rule: all of the grapes come from one vineyard and it is certainly a wonderful wine.

Parkton Prestige is a Bordeaux blend that's right on the mark. Angler Red and White are simple table wines that are easy to drink, but hard to beat. Woodhall really shines with its Cabernet Sauvignons. So deep and complex, the Reserve Cabernet makes a great addition to any cellar with its superb aging potential.

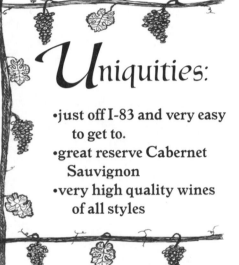

## *U*niquities:

- •just off I-83 and very easy to get to.
- •great reserve Cabernet Sauvignon
- •very high quality wines of all styles

"Wine is tough to grow, tough to make, and tough to sell," says cellar master, Chris Kent, who also works in the tasting room. "You have to really want to do it," he says. The owners and winemaker at Woodhall obviously live up to this statement.

Al Copp and Chris and Pat Lang are the owners while Copp and Ray Brasfield from Cygnus Winecellars are the winemakers. The Langs own the winery property and tend to the vineyards while everyone shares tasting room duty.

The tasting room is fairly large and can accomodate a good many people. There is no tasting bar, but rather two tall tables on which sit all Woodhall wines: one table for reds, one for whites. Someone is always there to answer questions and give you a tour of the winery. Take advantage of the opportunity to try these great wines, as most are from very limited productions.

# ine List

Seyval Blanc

Chardonnay

Angler White

Vidal Blanc

Riesling

Angler Red

Simply Red

Merlot

Parkton Prestige

Chambourcin

Cabernet Sauvignon

Copernica Reserve Cabernet Sauvignon

Late Harvest Vidal

# *R*ecipes

## Woodhall Venison Teriyaki

venison roast or steaks for two
1 cup Woodhall Cabernet Sauvignon        1/2 cup olive oil
2 tbsp teriyaki sauce                    1 tsp rosemary
2 cloves garlic, thinly sliced

Marinate venison (or beef) overnight.  Grill over charcoal or high heat until rare.  Enjoy with the rest of the Cabernet Sauvignon.

## Chicken Woodhall

one full chicken breast                  1/4 cup olive oil
1/4 tsp powdered garlic                  juice of 1/2 lemon
1/2 cup Woodhall Seyval or Chardonnay    six dashes of soy sauce

Combine all ingredients, except chicken, into a marinate.

Slice chicken breast into two or three slices per half breast the flat way (moderately thin).

Pour marinade over chicken slices and marinade ten minutes to overnight, depending on your mood and the time available!

Grill chicken quickly over high heat to just beyond pink stage. Reduce marinade slightly over heat and use as a sauce.

Enjoy with the rest of the Woodhall Seyval or Chardonnay.

*(These recipes were submitted by Al Copp of Woodhall Vineyards and Wine Cellars.)*

# Maryland Grape Growers

Maryland winemakers have an insatiable appetite for grapes. Both the amateur winemakers and the "Big 10" described in this book rely on independent grape growers to provide them with ample grapes.

Some of the independent growers in the state have less than one acre and provide grapes for local amateurs, while others have many more vines and cater more to the commercial wineries. Currently, more than 600 acres of grapes are being grown in Maryland.

Jack and Emily Johnston of Copernica Vineyards have five acres of vines at their site in Westminster. In 1998, 17 tons of grapes were harvested from their five acre vineyard including Pinot Blanc and Cabernet Sauvignon. Some of Copernica's best Cabernet Sauvignon grapes are used to make Woodhall's Copernica Cabernet Sauvignon Reserve.

Vineyards are springing up in just about every county in Maryland. They can be found from Garrett County in far western Maryland all the way east to Somerset and Caroline Counties on the eastern shore. There is excitement among grape growers and winemakers that the climate on the Eastern Shore is more conducive to vinifera grapes (like Chardonnay, Cabernet Sauvignon, and Merlot) that tend to have a difficult time surviving Maryland's harsh winters.

A grant was recently awarded to the Maryland Grape Growers Association to fund research and development for vineyards and a co-op winery on the Eastern Shore. Harry Smith, who grows grapes at his Coventry Parish Vineyard in Westover, feels the future of Maryland grape growing is on the Eastern Shore.

"The Eastern Shore is the place producing Maryland's finest Chardonnay now, and may be found to grow the best Italian wines as well," says Smith, who thinks the Eastern Shore could prove to be Maryland's best grape growing region.

He cites great reasons for starting a new branch of the Maryland wine and grape growing industry on the Eastern Shore. First of all, the region is buffered by the Chesapeake Bay and Atlantic Ocean, which provides a milder climate and growing season for grapes. Also, the Eastern Shore is already largely agricultural, so grape growing would be a perfect fit.

Smith points to the established tourism draw along the Route 50 and other corridors to Ocean City. Also, the Eastern Shore is home to some of the best cuisine in the country. The best blue crab, rock fish, oysters, wild duck and goose, and farm fresh produce combined with ancient culinary traditions make the Eastern Shore a perfect candidate for local wines!

Bill Kirby agrees with Smith. He's been growing grapes at his Wye Vineyard in Easton since April, 1984. Kirby started with Seyval, Chardonnay, and Cabernet Sauvignon and has more recently added Cabernet Franc and Merlot.

Kirby says when he stated he knew nothing about growing grapes. His involvement with the Maryland Grape Growers Association allowed him to learn from others' mistakes and gave him access to the experts of the time. He consulted with Ham Mowbray, John McGrew, Philip Wagner, and other "veterans of the vineyard learning curve."

*One of Maryland's vineyards.*

This is how most grape growers start out: knowing nothing and learning everything from area grape growers. Once established, a grape grower becomes an integral part of the Maryland wine industry, both commercial and amateur.

According to Muphen Whitney, Communications Director of the Association of Maryland Wineries, Maryland wineries could not survive without the independent grape growers.

"They're the underpinning of the Maryland wine industry, " says Whitney, citing the need for a good supply of grapes to meet the constant demand of the wineries.

There is, however, a great shortage of grapes every year. Not nearly enough acres of grapes are being grown in the state to support Maryland's winemaking needs. According to the Maryland Grape Growers Association (MGGA), in-state grape growers only supply 50 percent of the annual demand for grapes.

"Everyone who is growing grapes in Maryland today is selling all they can grow," Jim Russell, of Kingshill Vineyard says. He says wineries often have to buy out of state because they can't find enough Maryland grapes.

The MGGA encourages people to plant vines but warns that it is a tough field to go into. It can take up to seven years before a profit is seen, and that's only if the vines survive the first few years.

Robert Scott of Bellendine Vineyard in Carroll County says money isn't the most difficult aspect of starting a vineyard. "There wasn't a large investment to start up, but there was a lot of labor." He says it's much more labor than money.

Grape growing doesn't seem like a field to jump into full time. The financial rewards come years after the initial investment, and while much time is needed to start a vineyard, don't quit your day job just yet.

Robert Scott is an orthodontist for the better half of his time. And although he's taken great care to see that his vineyard is successful, it all comes together during his free time.

"Instead of playing golf, I pick grapes," says Scott. "I can really appreciate what a bottle of wine is like after all the hard work."

Ashley Vineyards owners Deb and Doug Alderson are making beautiful wine from their own grapes. Doug and his daughter Ashley had been making their own wine for the past few years, but now his wife Deb is getting involved in the process.

"We've had the opportunity to sell the grapes to other winemakers, but we're growing them for ourselves," says Doug Alderson, who is currently growing Chardonnay, Cabernet Sauvignon, and Cabernet Franc. Doug says while making wine is difficult, growing grapes is even harder.

Harder, perhaps, but well worth the effort. The rewards are not just financial. There is the wine that comes from the fruit of your labor and the many satisfied thanks that come from your customers.

More information can be had by contacting the
Maryland Grape Growers Association.
1116 E. Deep Run Road
Westminster, MD 21158
(410) 848-7577

# Mason-Dixon Wine Trail

And Noah, he often said to his wife
when he sat down to dine,
'I don't care where the water goes if it
doesn't get into the wine.'

—G. K. Chesterton

# Mason-Dixon Wine Trail

Maryland wines have so much to offer. Their styles are as unique as the winemakers who make them. Three of the northeasternmost Maryland wineries have joined forces with three of Pennsylvania's closest wineries to create the *"Mason-Dixon Wine Trail."*

Initiated by Mike Fiore of Fiore Winery and John Crouch of Pennsylvania's Allegro Vineyards in 1994, the wine trail gives consumers the opportunity to cross the border and try a few different styles and varieties of wines. The six wineries involved in the wine trail are Boordy, Fiore, and Woodhall in Maryland, and Allegro, Naylor, and Seven Valleys in Pennsylvania. The wineries are each about 20-30 minutes apart making it easy to try all six on one road trip. Be warned, though—all of the wines are great, so spend some time enjoying the scenery at each stop before heading to the next!

Be sure to pick up the wine trail information at your first stop, and make sure you ask for directions to the next winery—the owners encourage you to "taste around" and will guide you to the next closest winery on the trail. Most of the wineries have specials for wine trail trippers, including case discounts, giveaways, and occasional special events.

In this section, I will cover the Pennsylvania wineries on the wine trail. The Maryland wineries have been covered in the previous pages.

"Hey, this is a book about Maryland wineries, right?" Yes, indeed, but the three Pennsylvania wineries on the wine trail are so close and so distinctive, that it is well worth the extra pages to include them. Besides, if you're in the mood to visit even more wineries, ask what other Pennsylvania wineries are nearby.

# Map of Mason-Dixon
# Wine Trail Wineries

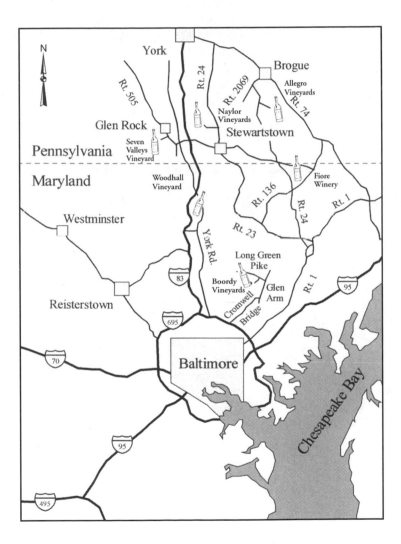

# ALLEGRO VINEYARDS

| | |
|---|---|
| Founded: | 1980 |
| Owners: | Tim and John Crouch |
| Winemaker: | John Crouch |
| Address: | RD 2, Box 64 |
| | Brogue, PA 17309 |
| Phone: | (717) 927-9148 |
| Hours: | 12 p.m - 5 p.m. daily. Closed major holidays. Large groups should call ahead. Tours and tastings are free. |
| Annual production: | 7,000 gallons |
| Price range of wines: | $6.50 to $25.00 |
| Amenities available: | Bathrooms, picnic areas. The winery is wheelchair accessible. |
| Area Wineries: | *"Mason-Dixon Wine Trail"* Wineries |
| Local attractions: | York, Lancaster |

John and Tim Crouch both love what they do. They've been in this business for a long time and have tons of stories and anecdotes to pass on. All of this while they pour their wines.

"Old vines make fine wines," says Tim Crouch. His Cabernet Sauvignon vines are 25 years old—the oldest in Pennsylvania. Allegro has won 80 medals in the last seventeen years.

Allegro has twelve acres of grapes on site including Seyval, Vidal, Chardonnay, Cabernet Sauvignon, Riesling, Merlot, Cabernet Franc, and others. What started as an amateur hobby has turned into an award-winning winery.

Michael Dresser of the Baltimore *Sun* said that Allegro's Cadenza is "One of the best red wines grown east of the Rockies." It's art, too. Each vintage gets a new label from a local artist and all are beautiful.

John and Tim host "Spotlight Weekends" and Chef Series events to celebrate their wines. They also hold a holiday open house where you can sample their wines and good cheer. Of their fifteen wines, around ten are regularly available for tasting. Allegro makes some really great wines.

Spend some time talking with John and Tim and ask them for

*Allegro's covered patio sits just in front of the winery making it a very convenient picnic spot.*

some suggestions as to what to do in the area while you're touring (and get directions to the other area wineries).

# ine List

Premium White

Vidal

Riesling

Chardonnay

Reserve Chardonnay

Celeste

Brogue Blush

Premium Red

Proprietor's Special Selection Red

Reserve Chambourcin

Cabernet Sauvignon

Cadenza

# Recipes

## Allegro Cheese Soup

6 green onions, thinly sliced
2 tsp olive oil
2/3 cup chopped cheddar cheese
2 1/2 cups water
1/4 tsp ground nutmeg
1 tsp dried basil
1/2 tsp black pepper

1 cup thinly sliced celery
2 tbsp butter
2/3 cup soft cooking cheese
1 cup cream
2/3 cup Seyval wine
1 tsp dried chives

Cook and stir green onions and celery in olive oil and melted butter. Use medium heat until onions and celery are tender (8-10 min). Stir in remaining ingredients except wine. Heat to boiling over medium heat, stirring often. Add wine and allow soup to boil for a minute. Sprinkle with paprika if desired, and serve.

(For croutons: air-popped popcorn with melted butter, olive oil, and grated Parmesan tossed together.)

## Potato Pie Allegro

2 - 9" unbaked pie shells
2 cups mashed potatoes (unseasoned)
1/2 cup thinly sliced spring onion
3 tsp grated Parmesan cheese

1 lb cottage cheese
1/2 cup sour cream
2 eggs lightly beaten
salt and pepper to taste

In a large bowl, beat mashed potatoes into cottage cheese. Beat in sour cream, eggs, salt and pepper. Mix in spring onions. Spoon into pie shells. Sprinkle tops with grated Parmesan cheese. Bake at 400° F for 40 minutes or until very golden brown on top. Allow to cool several minutes before cutting and serving.

Serve with Allegro Seyval or Premium White.

*(These recipes were submitted by John and Tim Crouch of Allegro Vineyards.)*

# NAYLOR VINEYARDS and WINE CELLARS

| | |
|---|---|
| Founded: | 1978 |
| Owners: | Richard and Audrey Naylor |
| Winemaker: | Ted Potter |
| Address: | 4069 Vineyard Rd. |
| | Stewartstown, PA 17363 |
| Phone: | (717) 993-2431, 1-800-292-3370 |
| Hours: | Monday thru Saturday 11 a.m.-6 p.m. and |
| | Sunday 12 p.m.-5 p.m. Tours and tastings |
| | are free. Large groups should call ahead. |
| Annual production: | 20,000 gallons |
| Price range of wines: | $6.45 to $25.00 |
| Amenities available: | Bathrooms, picnic areas. The winery is |
| | wheelchair accessible. |
| Area Wineries: | *"Mason-Dixon Wine Trail"* Wineries |
| Local attractions: | Wolfgang Candy, York, PA |

Naylor sits atop a hill on Vineyard Road. Very appropriate. This winery is making some of the best wines in Pennsylvania and with nearly thirty wines at any given time, you're bound to come away with more than a few bottles.

The tasting room is set amidst all the wine making equipment in the middle of the warehouse-like winery. Interesting gifts and brochures line the walls while bottles line the tasting bar.

Dick Naylor planted his first 1.25 acres of vines in 1975 and has been expanding ever since. He learned to make wine by taking weekend courses and reading every wine book he could get his hands on. Because of this, he strives to share his learned skills with anyone interested in becoming a part of the art of winemaking.

Naylor says he was happy to turn his winemaking duties over to son-in-law Ted Potter. "He's making much better wine than I ever did." Potter, a trained chef, makes a lot of wine—about 20,000 gallons a year—but all of it is of utmost quality. There isn't a bad wine among them! Potter believes that there should be a wine for everyone, and he's made that a reality.

If you plan it right (or call ahead to find out), you can attend

*A view of Naylor Vineyards and Wine Cellars from their event stage set in the woods behind the winery.*

one of their many summer concert events. Even if you've missed the event, walk back and check out the stage and picnic area overlooking the vineyards to see why it's also a favorite wedding spot!

# Wine List

York White Rose

Seyval

Vidal Perfection

Cabernet Sauvignon

Pinot Noir

Summertime Red

Barone IV

First Capital

Rhinelander

Niagara

Ekem

Catawba

Ambrosia's Dulce

Sugar Plum

# *R*ecipes

## Ted's Minestrone Aufena

| | |
|---|---|
| 1/4 lb bacon, diced | 1 onion, coarsely chopped |
| 2 cloves garlic, crushed | 5 cups water |
| 15 1/2 oz extra thick pasta sauce | 1/2 cup sliced carrots |
| 1 cup red wine (Naylor First Capital) | 1/2 cup sliced celery |
| 2 env. dehydrated beef broth | 1 large zucchini sliced |
| 1/2 tsp lemon pepper seasoning | 1 tsp salt |
| 1 can (1 lb) kidney beans | 1/2 cup small shell macaroni |
| 2 tbsp grated parmesan cheese | 1 tbsp chopped parsley |

In a dutch oven or large heavy saucepan, saute bacon until lightly browned. Stir in onions and garlic. Cook until onion is tender but not browned. Add pasta sauce and next eight ingredients, mixing well. Bring to boil, reduce heat to medium, cover, and cook for one hour. Stir once or twice. Add kidney beans and macaroni. Simmer 15 minutes longer. Garnish with parsley and grated cheese. Serves 8.

## Naylor Chili con Corde

| | |
|---|---|
| 1 lb of lean ground beef | 1 tbsp chili powder |
| 3 medium onions, coarsely chopped | 1 can (40 oz) kidney beans |
| 2 cans (28 oz ea.) diced tomatoes | 1 cup Naylor Concord Wine |
| 1/2 oz unsweetened baking chocolate | |

In a 4 qt. heavy saucepan, brown ground beef over medium heat, breaking up lumps with a spoon. When meat is almost browned, add onions and chili powder and stir well. Cook until meat is browned and onions are soft. Add kidney beans, wine, tomatoes, and chocolate. Stir well. Bring to boil over high heat and simmer until mixture is the desired thickness (20-30 min). Serve in soup bowls and garnish with shredded cheddar. Makes 10 cups.

*(These recipes were submitted by Ted Potter of Naylor Vineyards and Wine Cellars.)*

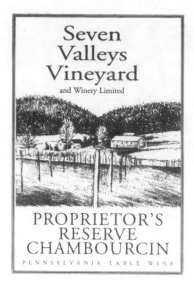

# SEVEN VALLEYS VINEYARD and WINERY

Founded:               1994
Owners:                Fred and Lynn Hunter
Winemaker:             Fred Hunter
Address: ***           885 Georges Court
                       Glen Rock, PA 17327
Phone:                 (717) 235-6281
Hours:                 Saturdays and Sundays 10-5 p.m.  Tours
                       and tastings are free.  Large groups should
                       call ahead.
Annual production:     2,500 gallons
Price range of wines:  $7.50 to $13.00
Amenities available:   Bathrooms, picnic areas overlooking a scenic
                       pond.
Area Wineries:         *"Mason-Dixon Wine Trail"* Wineries
Local attractions:     Town of Shrewsbury has many antique
                       shops, cafes, and a great italian restaurant.

***Seven Valleys does have a wine shop in Shrewsbury, Pennsylvania, located at 27 N. Main Street.  It's open Wednesdays and Thursdays 11-6 p.m., Fridays and Saturdays 11-7 p.m. and Sundays 12-6 p.m. The wine shop's number is (717) 227-0257

Owners Lynn and Fred Hunter are simply as wonderful as their wine. Their personalities are enough to keep customers coming back again and again. But their wines seal the deal.

Their winery has blossomed over the years into one of the best kept secrets of the Pennsylvania wine industry. In fact, Lynn says that, for some reason, people who have tried their wine act like they've been exposed to a secret to be kept all to themselves.

"There seems to be this legend about our winery," says Lynn, as she describes people whispering to her about her own wine as if it's a huge secret. "I think we're turning into a cult winery." There's nothing wrong with that!

The fans have nothing to worry about. The Hunter's wines are all wonderful, and they have a great variety to suit just about any palate. Fred Hunter is the winemaker, and he's been practicing his art for a long time. He began as a home winemaker, planting grapes in 1976, but decided to open the winery in 1994.

There are 25 acres of vines at Seven Valleys Vineyard consisting of Gewürztraminer, Vidal, Chancellor, Steuben, Seyval, Cabernet Sauvigon, Riesling, Chambourcin, Cayuga, and Chardonnay.

The Hunters do not use all of their grapes on their own wine. Seven Valleys grapes are sold to a number of Maryland wineries. Their grapes go in to some of Maryland's best wine.

"My goal is to make the best wine from the best grapes we can grow," Lynn Hunter says. She insists that great wines can only come from great grapes. She needn't worry—her wine is superb and should be a staple for anyone interested in spectacular regional wine.

If you can't make it to the winery on the weekend, stop by their wine shop in the town of Shrewsbury. It's an attractive store with a tasting bar and a variety of gifts for sale.

# Wine List

Seyval

Proprietor's White

Vidal Blanc

Limerick

Late Harvest Vidal

Riesling

Country Red

Cabernet Sauvignon

Steuben Blush

Chambourcin

Gewürztraminer

Celebration

Country White

# *R*ecipes

## Linguine with Braised Garlic and Balsamic Vinegar from the Splendid Table

3 tbsp extra-virgin olive oil or unsalted butter
8 large cloves garlic, cut into 1/4-inch dice
3 tbsp extra-virgin olive oil or unsalted butter
Salt and freshly ground black pepper to taste
1 to 1-1/2 cups (4 to 6 ounces) freshly grated Italian Parmigiano-Reggiano cheese
8 to 10 tsps artisan-made or high-quality commercial balsamic vinegar
    (if using commercial, blend in 1 teaspoon brown sugar)

6 quarts salted water
1 lb imported dried linguine

Braising the garlic:  In a large heavy skillet, heat the 3 tablespoons oil or butter over medium-low heat.  Add the garlic, and lower the heat to the lowest possible setting.  Cook, covered, 5 minutes.  Uncover and continue cooking over the lowest possible heat 8 minutes, or until the garlic is barely colored to pale blond and very tender.  Stir it frequently with a wooden spatula.  Do not let the garlic turn medium to dark brown, as it will be bitter.

Cooking the pasta:  Warm a serving bowl and shallow soup dishes in a low oven.  As the garlic braises, bring the salted water to a fierce boil, and drop in the pasta.  Stir occasionally.  Cook up to 10 minutes for dried pasta.  Taste for doneness, making sure the pasta is tender but still firm to the bite.  Spoon about 3 tablespoons of the cooking water into the cooked garlic just before draining the pasta.  Drain in a colander.

Finishing and serving:  Remove the garlic from the heat and add the hot drained pasta.  Add the additional 3 tablespoons of oil or butter (the fresh taste of uncooked oil or butter brightens the dish), and toss with two wooden spatulas.  Season with salt and pepper.  Now toss with all of the cheese.  Turn into the heated serving bowl.  As you serve the pasta, sprinkle each plateful with a teaspoon or so of the vinegar.  Serves 6 to 8 as a first course, 4 to 6 as a main dish.

Serve with Seven Valleys Proprietor's White.

*(This recipe was donated by Lynne Rossetto Kasper, host of the public radio program, The Spendid Table.  It can also be found in* The Splendid Table: Recipes from Emilia-Romagna, the Heartland of Northern Italian Food *by Lynne Rossetto Kasper, William Morrow and Company, Inc., 1992.)*

# Good Information

When there is plenty of wine, sorrow
and worry take wing.

—Ovid, 'The Art of Love'

# Wine Festivals

Wine festivals provide a great opportunity for wine lovers. For a fee, you get to try lots of wine while listening to music and eating great food! And, if you're interested in volunteering at one of the wineries' tents, let them know—they always need help!

The festivals listed below are just a start! Many of the wineries hold their own events, celebrating new wine releases or just about any excuse to invite people over for a good time. Ask when you visit, or pick up a "Wines of Maryland Calendar of Events" which can be found at each winery.

These dates and events may change, so check with the Association of Maryland Wineries at 1-800-237-WINE or check their website at www.marylandwine.com for more information.

**May:**
Wine in the Woods, Symphony Woods, Howard County, usually the second or third weekend of May, 410-313-7275.

**June:**
Chesapeake Wine and Beer Fest, usually held the second weekend in June as a benefit for Baltimore Area Retarded Citizens (BARC), 410-296-2272.

**September:**
Maryland Wine Festival, Carroll County Farm Museum, Westminster, usually the third weekend in September, 1-800-654-4645
> This event has been named one of the five best events of its kind in North America by "Tours" Magazine. All of the Maryland wineries join food vendors, musicians, artists, and crafters in two days of fun and educational events including winetasting classes. Also, the results of the Governor's Cup wine awards are announced here!

# Wine Associations

These associations are good resources for anyone interested in wine, grapes, and the industry as a whole.

American Institute of Wine and Food
1-800-274-AIWF, National Office
Baltimore Chapter (410) 244-0044

American Wine Society
(716) 225-7613
Call for information on local chapters.

Association of Maryland Wineries
1-800-237-WINE
www.marylandwine.com

Maryland Grape Growers Association
1116 E. Deep Run Road
Westminster, MD 21158
(410) 848-7577

*Gary Griggs, member of the American Wine Society, conducts a tasting at the Maryland Wine Festival.*

# Wine Publications

## Magazines:
*Wine Enthusiast* 1-800-356-8466
*Wine Spectator* 1-800-395-3364
> Both of these magazines offer reviews of wines and informative articles and columns about wine, wine regions around the world, and general wine appreciation.

## Books:
*Oz Clarke's Wine Atlas.* Oz Clarke.
New York: Little, Brown and Company, 1995.
> The definitive atlas of all of the major wine regions with pictures, maps, and very good explanations of the wines and grapes grown in each region.

*The University Wine Course.* Marion W. Baldy.
San Francisco: Wine Appreciation Guild, 1997.
> This is a college text, but it provides wonderful information in a very smart format for anyone interested in furthering their knowledge of wines and winemaking.

*Wine for Dummies.* Ed McCarthy. Mary Ewing-Mulligan.
Foster City, CA: IDG Books International, 1995.
> You can't go wrong with this book if you want an introduction to wine. It's written very simply and is a great help for beginning wine drinkers.

*Wineries of the Eastern States.* Marguerite Thomas.
Lee, MA: Berkshire House Publishers, 1997.
> This book gives an overview of the wine regions on the Eastern Seaboard while highlighting a few wineries in each state.

*Winetaster's Secrets.* Andrew Sharp.
Los Angeles, CA: Warwick Publishing, 1995.
> If you want to know many tricks of winetasters, here's your book. Sharp takes great care to describe most grape varieties, their characteristics and how to identify them.

# Where to Buy Maryland Wines

As of this book's printing, Maryland laws prohibit the wineries from shipping wine directly to consumers. This means that each winery must go through a distributor to make their wines available to the general public. Although this law is extremely antiquated, it gives consumers good reason to visit and revisit their favorite wineries.

Otherwise, here are the best ways to find Maryland wines:

1. The easiest way to get your favorite Maryland wines is to purchase directly from the winery. If you find something you like, buy it by the case at the winery because most will give a 10-20 percent discount on all case purchases.

2. Buy from the wineries at one of the annual festivals. This is a great opportunity to try many wines and buy as much as you like in one trip.

3. Buy from your local wine merchant. Most of the Maryland wines are distributed throughout the area, especially in the larger wine and liquor stores. When you visit, ask the wineries if their wines are available in your area.

*Newly bottled Basignani Lorenzino Reserve awaits sale in the tasting room.*

# Useful Wine Terms

**ACIDITY** - the essential natural element that gives wine its crispness on the palate. Too much and the wine will seem hard or bitter. Too little and the wine will seem flabby.

**AFTERTASTE** - the taste left in the mouth (good or bad) after the wine has been swallowed.

**AROMA** - the fragrance of the grape. What the winemaker does and the winemaking techniques used evolve into nuances of smell that are called "bouquet."

**BALANCE** - the harmony of all a wine's components—sugar, fruit, tannin, wood, and alcohol. Wines where one or more component stands out and dominates the wine are considered out of balance.

**COMPLEX** - one of the most subjective descriptive terms used, a complex wine should have lots of different smells and flavors that seem to change with each sip.

**DEPTH** - wine with depth has a concentration of flavors, a rich intensity, and tends to be mouth-filling.

**DRY** - the opposite of sweet. A wine is dry when all of the sugar in the grapes has been fermented into alcohol. The acid content may also determine the sense of dryness.

**FINISH** - the aftertaste, also called length. All wine has a finish, whether it is short or long, pleasant or unpleasant. A long and/or pleasant finish is preferable to a short and/or unpleasant finish.

**HYBRID** - a mix between a hardier native American grape variety and one of European descent.

**FRUITY** - conveying an impression of fruit, sometimes grapes, but often other kinds of fruit, including raspberries, peaches, apricots, cherries, black currants, etc. A fruity wine can be completely dry, with no residual sugar.

**FULL-BODIED** - wines rich in grape extract, alcohol, and glycerine are full-bodied.

**SOFT** - describes a wine lacking the bite of tannins or acids

**SULFITES** - when a label reads "Contains Sulfites," it means sulfur dioxide was used in the process of grape growing or winemaking. Persons allergic to sulfites should be cautious when choosing their wines.

**SWEET** - one of the four basic tastes perceived by the tongue, as opposed to the hundreds of flavors that we actually experience with our olfactory senses. The presence of sugar (or occasionally of glycerine) is required to taste sweetness.

**TANNIN** - one of the key acids found in wine. It comes from the skins, seeds, and stems of the grapes. This is what makes your mouth pucker when drinking a red wine, especially a young one. Tannin is what gives wine its longevity and dryness.

**VARIETAL** - a wine made from at least 75 percent of one grape variety.

**VINIFERA** *(Vitis Vinifera)* - 99 percent of all wines are made from this grape species. There are thousands of varieties of this species, most notably Chardonnay, Cabernet Sauvignon, Merlot, Pinot Noir, Riesling, and Zinfandel.

**VINTAGE** - the year of a harvest and when the wine was made.

*(Thanks to Corridor Wine & Spirits in Laurel, MD for supplying some of the above terms.)*

# Order Form

Name:_____

Address:_____

_____

City:_____State:_____Zip:_____

Phone:_____E-mail:_____

☐ *Please add my name to your mailing list.*

**Please send me:**

_____ copies of *Discovering Maryland Wineries*
     by Kevin Atticks  $9.95/each

_____ copies of *From This Hill, My Hand, Cynthiana's Wine*
     by Paul Roberts  $16.95/each

_____ copies of *Discovering Lake Erie Wineries*
     by Kevin Atticks  $11.95/each

Understand that you may return all books within 30 days for a full refund – no questions asked if books are in good shape.

**Shipping:**
Please add $1.50 for each book to cover shipping and handling.

**Payment:**
Cash, checks, and money orders are accepted.  Please make checks payable to resonant publishing and send to the address listed below.

*Send all inquiries to:*

**resonant ◉ publishing**

PMB 179  •  211 E. Lombard St.  •  Baltimore, MD 21202
info@resonantgroup.com  •  www.resonantgroup.com